CW00329560

The Art of Managing

In affectionate memory of
Sir Adrian Cadbury, 1929–2015,
without whom the world of business and
management would be a much poorer place.

The Art of
Managing

JOHN HENDRY

ROBERT HALE

First published in 2016 by Robert Hale,
an imprint of The Crowood Press Ltd,
Ramsbury, Marlborough Wiltshire SN8 2HR

www. crowood.com

www.halebooks.com

© John Hendry 2016

All rights reserved. No part of this publication may be
reproduced or transmitted in any form or by any means,
electronic or mechanical, including photocopy, recording
or any information storage and retrieval system, without
permission in writing from the publishers.

British Library Cataloguing-in-Publication Data
A catalogue record for this book is available from the British
Library.

ISBN 978 0 7198 1895 0

The right of John Hendry to be identified as author of this
work has been asserted by him in accordance with the
Copyright, Designs and Patents Act 1988.

Typeset by Jean Cussons Typesetting, Diss, Norfolk

Printed and bound in India by Replika Press Pvt Ltd

Contents

Preface and Acknowledgements

Much of my career has been back to front, and when I first taught management, at the London Business School in the mid-1980s, I had neither studied it myself nor acquired much in the way of management experience. I have since rectified both failings, but meanwhile I had the great good fortune to be allocated an office next-door to Charles Handy. Charles had both practised and studied managing, and after a brief interlude in academe was to become, arguably, our best writer on the challenges it poses. With characteristic kindness he took me under his wing and taught me several important lessons. First, that we all manage, all the time, whether or not we are called 'managers'. Second, that the best way to learn is by doing, and the best aid to learning is responsibility. Third, that contrary to the teaching of many of our colleagues, the key to good management lay less in specialist knowledge and expertise, and more in common sense, thoughtfulness, imagination and the simple ability to treat people as people, and to treat them well.

I was also lucky in that one of the first managers whose work I seriously studied was Sir Peter Parker, best known for his enlightened chairmanship of British Railways in the late 1970s and early 1980s, who followed very much the same principles. Both he and Charles were great enthusiasts, as indeed am I, for management theory, and both were pioneers in the advancement of management education. But both were, first and foremost, deeply caring and thoughtful human beings, who believed passionately in people's innate ability and creativity. They thought that management should be taken much more seriously than it then was in Britain, and that formal management education was a way of exciting people to take it seriously. But they saw such an education as helping people to ask questions – not as giving them answers. Coming from relatively privileged backgrounds, they also saw particular importance in the advancement of elite management education, at places like the London Business School, as a way of getting management taken seriously in the upper reaches of society, where it had traditionally been despised and neglected. But they were not at all elitist themselves. Both believed firmly, on the basis of their own management experience, not only that people from all backgrounds should be valued and respected as equals, but also that they were typically much more talented and capable than they were given credit for.

In the years that followed I discovered that the Handy–Parker model was the exception rather than the rule. As management education expanded, it came to be seen as a substitute for real managing, not as an aid. And as people sang the praises of leadership and entrepreneurship, the art of managing continued to be neglected. I also found, however, that when the model was adopted, in whatever kind or size of organization and at whatever level, the outcome was almost always positive. Moreover, people didn't have to be that brilliant at managing to make it work. With some effort and attention, a bit of thought, a bit of common sense and a bit of compassion, almost anybody could manage pretty well. I could even do it myself!

This book is dedicated to all those people, wherever they may be, in whatever circumstances and whatever walk of life, who try their honest best to manage. It's not always easy, and it's rarely appreciated as much as it should be, but managing matters. It matters a lot.

I am particularly conscious of the teachers, colleagues and bosses, friends and relations, who have had the unenviable task of trying to manage me. Some have been superb, and I have learnt a lot from them, as well as from the many, many managers I've taught, advised or observed in action. A very few of the colleagues and bosses have been quite awful, and I've learnt a lot from them too, about how managing badly or without good intentions can literally ruin people's lives. Again, managing really matters.

I'm also very grateful to the people who have found themselves subject, in one way or another, to my own efforts at managing. It goes without saying that I have not always managed to manage in accordance with my own advice, and reading back over the book I still wince slightly when particular guidelines bring to mind the things I could and should have done better. But I smile, too, at the kindness and understanding people have shown in such cases.

For making this book possible, I should like especially to thank Dee, my wife, for her usual tolerance of a writer's antisocial habits, and Robert Hale Ltd, who approached me out of the blue just when I was formulating the idea and have courageously stuck by the outcome. Finally, I should also like to pay my respects to one of the great managers of the twentieth century, Adrian Cadbury, who died just as this manuscript was being submitted. Chairman of the well-known chocolate company, managing director and chairman of Cadbury Schweppes, and pioneer of corporate governance and ethical business, Adrian combined firm management and a hard-headed approach to business with true humility and exemplary humanity. He was a lesson to us all.

London, October 2015

Introduction

This is a book for anyone whose job includes some element of management, which I shall define in practical terms as exercising responsibility for the work of other people. You may or may not be called a manager. The task of managing goes under a variety of names; job titles can be misleading or uninformative, and management may be just a small part of what you do. Even if it is only a small part, however, it is likely to be an important one, and the challenges it poses are quite different from those posed by other kinds of work.

People come to managing from a wide variety of backgrounds and with a wide variety of experience, training, ambition and expectations. For many self-employed tradespeople and professionals, for the owners of small firms and even for people promoted to head up specialist teams or departments, the task of managing assistants or administrators may be an unwanted hassle. Chefs, for example, love to cook, but with the freedom to cook their own way comes the responsibility of managing a kitchen, and many find that irksome.

Even where a management role is much more welcome, as a recognition of achievement and promotion up the corporate ladder, it can be very daunting. People appointed to their first management position can often feel lost or confused, with no clear job description, no fixed hours and, in many cases, little or no training or guidance. They want to succeed, but they don't know how to go about it, or what's expected of them. A management role can also tear you away from your colleagues: even though your values and motives remain unchanged, you suddenly become part of 'them' ('the management') rather than 'us'.

In larger organizations, many people appointed to management roles will have received some training, either through attending a business school or through some equivalent in-house courses. This is at best a mixed blessing, however, for while business schools can teach you all sorts of fascinating facts and theories, that won't necessarily help you to manage any better. Indeed, it can easily do more harm than good. Management theories start out from assumptions about human behaviour and motivation. They then derive prescriptions for how to manage, based on those assumptions. This would be all very well if the assumptions were anything like realistic, but they're not. They're very simplistic and in many contexts quite inappropriate – and so are the prescriptions based upon them.

This is not to say that the study of management theories is worthless. So long as we keep in mind their limitations, they can give us all sorts of valuable insights, both to the challenges of management and to the way those challenges are addressed, especially in large organizations. The procedures and practices of many large organizations are based on management theories developed by academics and consultants and taught in business schools, and we can only understand those procedures and practices if we know something about the theories behind them. Whatever the business schools might claim, however, management is much more of an art than a science.

In an earlier book, *Management: A Very Short Introduction*, I tried to survey the literature on management theory in such a way as to make it useful and interesting to practising managers, as well as to business school students. But you don't need to know about management theory to be a good manager, and in this book the focus is entirely on the practice or art of managing. The guidance offered is informed by theory and makes use of the many lessons learned by management consultants and academics over the years. But it is mainly based on common sense, experience and the kinds of principles that will reap rewards, if carefully applied, in any context in which we have to make a success out of living and working together.

Good management brings with it all sorts of benefits. It benefits the managers themselves, by making their work more rewarding, advancing their careers and giving them a platform for growth and development. It benefits the people being managed, by making their work more rewarding and more enjoyable. We all work most effectively when we enjoy what we are doing, when going into the workplace lifts up our spirits rather than dampening them. And, of course, it benefits the organization, through improved productivity all round. My main focus in this book is on you, the manager, but everything here applies equally to any managers who report to you, and to any of your staff who may be managers in the future. Many of the skills that make up the art of managing can only be applied through managing. But many others can be developed in any job, and the attitudes and values that underpin them can be developed in any context whatsoever, at any time.

The book is divided into three parts. In the first part (Chapters 1 and 2), I explore the manager's job: what is managing and what does it entail? A central theme of the book is that management is as much about coping as controlling – like when we say, in the midst of domestic chaos, 'I'm managing'. It's also as much about leadership as about administration – and as much about administration as about leadership. Both are important parts of the job. Two other important elements are trouble-shooting, or sorting things out when they go wrong, and coaching, or helping the people who work under you to work more effectively, and perhaps to become managers themselves.

In the second part (Chapter 3), I set out fifty guidelines for effective managing, each in the form of a simple principle or maxim and a short account of how and why it matters. Some of these principles can be traced back hundreds or thousands of years. Some reflect the wisdom built up in more recent years, as management jobs have proliferated and the challenges posed have been systematically analysed and explored. Some are drawn from my own experience of managing, helping others to manage and mining the experience of successful managers for the benefit of my students. These guidelines are not always easy to apply, and you shouldn't be put off if you find some of them too ambitious or too idealistic. They are things to work at rather than things to be achieved, and if you can only work at them a little bit at a time, that's fine. Start with what comes most easily and set yourself tougher challenges when you're ready.

In the third part (Chapters 4–7), I give a very short introduction to the essential tools and techniques of managing. This comes closer to the kind of content you will find in a management textbook, but with the important difference that the sole criterion for inclusion is practical utility. You can find many more complete guides, along the lines of '100 essential tools for managers', but the fact is that many tools and techniques sold as essential are not really very useful at all, or are much more useful to specialist analysts than to practising managers. And some of the most useful are passed over, either because they're too basic or because they don't have a catchy label and nobody has tried to 'sell' them.

This part of the book is the most technically demanding, and if you've had no exposure to management tools and techniques before, you may find parts of it hard to follow. Again, don't worry. Everything covered is potentially useful, but none of it is strictly necessary. You may find some things here that you want to learn more about, and if that's the case, you can go to Wikipedia and other internet sources, or to standard management textbooks, for fuller explanations. In other cases you might just lodge in the back of your mind that there's something there that might come in useful someday, but not worry about it too much for the time being.

Alongside the main text of Chapters 1–3, I have included a series of boxed examples of managing drawn from the experiences of ordinary managers. I have also drawn on these same examples to explain and illustrate some of the tools covered in Chapters 4–7. Managers are often unsung heroes, and to take examples from the management experiences of those who are known for their entrepreneurial prowess, or for their financial or political success, would be misleading. The managers I have used here are fictional composites, made up from some of those I have worked with as teacher, consultant or colleague. In that sense they are not 'real' but their situations and experiences are very real and they help to put some flesh on the issues raised.

CHAPTER 1

The Manager's Job

ARE YOU A MANAGER?

Some managers are called managers. You may be a shop manager, a floor manager or an office manager; a marketing manager, a sales manager or a production manager; a general manager, a managing partner or a managing director; or just a plain manager. In all these cases it's pretty evident that you are a manager.

Most managers, however, are not formally labelled as such. Supervisors of manual and clerical staff are conventionally denied managerial status, just as in the armed forces, corporals, sergeants and other non-commissioned officers are denied full officer status. But both supervisors and sergeants are clearly responsible for managing the people under their supervision. Hospital matrons occupy a similar position. Also, sitting below the formal management of an organization but very much involved in managing are many people who combine limited managerial responsibilities with their regular, non-management jobs. The current fashion is to call these people 'leaders', as in team leaders, project leaders or, in education, subject-group leaders, all of which is nicely ironic considering that many writers on leadership place it above 'mere' management.

A common catch-all job title is 'executive' or, in the civil service, 'executive officer'. This is sometimes used as a term to distinguish professional or graduate jobs from those requiring lower level qualifications, so that junior executives may have less managerial responsibilities than senior clerical or semi-skilled staff. But most executives are managers for at least part of their jobs, and 'executive programmes' in business schools are generally programmes for practising managers.

Higher up the organizational hierarchy, managers may be called 'directors' or 'vice-presidents', or hold one of the many officer ranks in the armed forces, police and other services. We also find 'heads' and 'chiefs' of one kind or another: section head, head of department, head teacher, chief accountant, chef and so on. And we also find deputy directors and deputy heads, many of whom share in the managerial responsibilities of their principals.

Finally, there are the many self-employed tradesmen, professionals and owners of small businesses who employ assistants of one kind or another: secretaries, receptionists, apprentices, accountants, employees in their own trades and professions, and so on. As we noted in the Introduction, management is not always a welcome part of a person's responsibilities, but it is a necessary and important one. No business or professional practice will flourish if it is not well-managed.

What all managerial roles have in common is some responsibility for the work of other people. This may just be a kind of overseeing but, even at a junior level, it usually involves some scheduling and allocation of duties. It typically involves helping people to learn their jobs and to do them better, monitoring and feedback, appraisal, and some contribution to hiring and firing and promotion decisions. It also involves some element of planning and of dealing with things when something happens to prevent them from working as planned: responding to illness and absence, to unexpected events, and to mistakes, and stepping in when someone is unable to deal with a situation – with a difficult or abusive customer, say.

This is just a beginning, of course. Managing can involve much more and, when done well, it does involve much more. But it is enough to start us off. If your job entails any of these things, to any extent at all – you are a manager.

ARE YOU MANAGING?

You are a manager, but are you managing? This question can be taken in two ways. In the context of a book on management, the most obvious meaning is, 'Are you engaging in managerial activities?'; but in any other context the meaning would be more like, 'Are you coping?'. It's a question we might ask someone with a leg in plaster, or an elderly person living alone, or a young mother with twin toddlers. Similarly, if we ask someone, in the usual way, how they are, and we get the response, 'Oh, I'm managing', we don't imagine that they've got a new job or taken some kind of managerial approach to the housework and shopping. We take it that they're finding things difficult but are 'managing to cope', one way or another.

Again, if we ask someone, 'How are you managing?' or 'How do you manage?', we don't normally expect to hear about the tools and techniques of management. A typical response would be, 'I get by', 'I cope' or some other vague reassurance, but if we do elicit anything more specific, it will probably be about the aids that help them get from one day to the next: 'People are very helpful' or 'Lucy gives me a hand in the mornings.'

This everyday meaning of managing is not something you'll find mentioned in most management courses or textbooks. Management there is all about planning and control. In practice, however, coping and control are just two ends of a spectrum. And just as managing in everyday life always entails a bit of both, so does managerial work. To assume that it could never get beyond coping would be defeatist. But to imagine that it was all about controlling would be to enter a world of fantasy. You must always keep both ends of the spectrum in mind.

We can get a further insight into this by thinking about how we use the word 'control'. To control things is to make sure they happen in the way you planned and intended, and this is certainly something that managers seek to do, even if they rarely achieve it. But as well as controlling, in an active sense, we also talk more passively about 'being in control' or 'staying in control', and this often carries with it a hint – or more than a hint – that things might easily slip out of control. It is somewhere between swimming strongly and just staying afloat, between walking the dog and being walked by it, and it is where managers often find themselves. In such a situation, the first priority is to master the current or secure your footing. Only then can you think about getting anywhere.

If controlling represents the glamorous, macho side of managing, administration represents its more mundane and supposedly boring side. Many writers have distinguished management, seen as routine administration, from leadership, seen as something far grander, far more glamorous and far harder to achieve. It is leaders we turn to for direction and inspiration, they suggest; managers just keep the wheels turning.

When we think of leaders, we tend to think of people in particular roles, for which this distinction makes sense. In politics, for example, there is a clear demarcation between the roles of elected politicians, who frame policies and sell those policies to the public, and salaried civil servants, who execute those policies. The politicians are, by necessity, in the public eye, and those who become known for their leadership do so on the basis of 'leadership' qualities that are evident to everyone. The civil servants, in contrast, are anonymous. In other contexts too, leadership is generally associated with some kind of popular appeal. The label comes with glamour attached – so much so, indeed, that we almost never talk of a failed leader. You can be a manager and fail, but if you fail in an attempt to lead, you just don't merit being called a leader at all.

It is easy to see, then, how the distinction between leadership and management might be made, but in most contexts it is deeply misleading. If we define leadership as a role or activity, rather than as an achievement, all managers have to lead. It is an essential part of the job. And anyone whose job includes an element of leadership is almost certainly a manager. Routine administration, meanwhile, is also an essential part of any manager's – or leader's – job, and in no way an inferior part. Some managers do find it boring; others find it very rewarding. But if it is not done both effectively (so that what needs to be done is done) and efficiently (so that other things can get done too), then things are likely to fall apart.

Somewhere between leadership and administration, and entailing elements of both, lie two other facets of managing that are worth noting explicitly. One is trouble-shooting. However effective your administration, things will go wrong. The people who work for you will make mistakes, or fall out, or be incapacitated by illness or personal problems. You will make mistakes. Your bosses will make mistakes. Customers will make unexpected demands, suppliers will fail to deliver and so on. As a manager, you will sometimes have to take charge and sort things out.

The other facet, often neglected, is coaching. An important part of any manager's job is helping the people who work for you to do their jobs better and to gain the skills and understanding they will need to progress their own careers. To some extent this should be part of your routine. If people are trying to improve and learn, they will need someone to share their issues and problems with, on a regular basis. If they are not trying to improve and learn, they will need someone to keep encouraging them to do so. You should also make use of particular situations, however, such as minor problems or one-off projects, to find ways of stretching people's capabilities and supporting them in the process.

A final facet of management to be covered in this part of the book is accountability. As a manager you will generally be held accountable, at least in part, for the work of the people you manage. Sometimes you will be held to account. You will have to give an account to your superiors of why something went wrong or why a performance target was missed, including why it happened on your watch and what you will do to improve things in the future. Even when you are not called to account, however, you will remain accountable and this will necessarily impact on other aspects of your job.

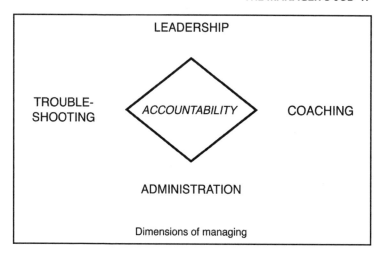

Dimensions of managing

This applies most obviously to professionals, like doctors, accountants or solicitors, who are very strictly accountable, both legally and professionally, for anything done under their nominal supervision, and who have to take care appropriately. It evidently applies also to the owners of small businesses. In other contexts the accountability may be much less explicit, but good managers always assume it's there. They act, in this respect, as if they were professionals.

WHAT ARE YOU MANAGING?

The words 'managing' and 'management' derive from a Latin term for the art of handling a horse: getting it to go where you want to, at the speed you want it to – to walk, trot, canter, gallop, jump, turn or stand still – and to execute the kind of movements you see in dressage events. This was extended over time to handling weapons, boats and eventually people, and it is the origin of the connotation of control. An expert rider seeks to control a horse, not just to stay seated.

Managing a horse is not easy, but it has at least one advantage when compared with the kind of activity we're talking about here: you know what you are managing. It's a horse and, in particular, the physical movements of the horse. Managing an office, or a department, or a business or a project is evidently more complicated. There are likely to be many end-products of various different kinds: physical, financial and psychological. To achieve them you will need to manage, in some sense, people's thoughts, feelings and perceptions, as well as their actions, the interactions between different people, and the interactions between people and physical and IT processes.

We can get a handle on this complexity by dividing what is to be managed into two categories on each of two dimensions. In the first place, we can distinguish between managing what goes on inside the unit for which you are responsible and managing what happens across its boundaries, whether with other units in the organization or with customers, suppliers and other external stakeholders. In the second place we can distinguish between the task of managing people and that of managing information.

Neither of these distinctions is clear-cut, but making them helps us to focus clearly on particular aspects of what is being managed that might otherwise be neglected. For example, some managers turn their units into tightly bonded teams with strong cultures and high levels of loyalty and ownership. This can be great for building performance within the unit, but it can make things very difficult for the other units with which it has to interact. And it is all too easy to attribute blame for these difficulties, quite unfairly, to the other units. So a manager building a strong team has to attend very carefully to how that team interacts with others. Similarly, in reverse, managers who focus strongly on how their units can serve others, whether inside or outside the organization, and on what they can pull in from others – both valid and valuable objectives – can easily lose sight of the dynamics of the units themselves.

In the case of the other distinction, the tasks of managing people and managing information obviously overlap, but the skills required

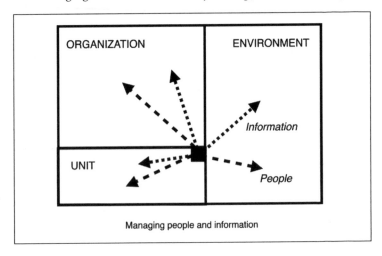

Managing people and information

can be very different. So if you need to give people information – about the organization, its environment or their own performance – you need to be very careful how you give it. All facts are prone to interpretation and what you present as an opportunity may be received as a nuisance or a threat. If the personal side isn't managed carefully, the simplest of facts can become the basis for wild and unhelpful speculation. On the other hand, managers who focus strongly on interpersonal relationships risk holding back information that is actually needed, when they think it might be troubling.

When it comes to managing across organizational boundaries, again, both people and information skills matter. Some managers take the view that so long as they do a technically good job, it doesn't matter how well or how badly they get on with their colleagues and superiors. They are wrong! Quite apart from the impacts on their own careers, poor interpersonal skills on the part of one manager are costly for everyone else, and so for the organization as a whole.

Some managers focus all their effort, when managing upwards or outwards, on the interpersonal side, and neglect the core task, which is to act as an information gateway. A unit relies on its manager to monitor, sort, filter and pass on information about the world outside it, in particular about where the organization is headed, what the priorities are and what is expected of it. The rest of the organization relies on the manager for information about the unit, about the challenges it is facing, the support it might need from elsewhere and the contributions it might make. Again this has to be filtered, sorted and presented in a concise and useful way. All this entails people skills, as well as information skills. A lot of information is conveyed informally and, to keep abreast, managers need to be good networkers. But they need to network for a purpose, not to let it dominate their working lives.

HOW ARE YOU MANAGING?

The problem of how to manage is also much simpler in the case of a horse than in the case of an organization. You manage a horse through physical contact and pressure, systematically applied. This is not to be recommended for managing people, and won't get you very far in managing information either. To a very large extent, managers manage through the much more complex medium of language. They speak and listen, write and read. They also think. And they sometimes act.

To a business school student, management is largely a question of thinking. Management students are presented with problems and instructed in the frameworks and techniques with which to analyse them. The challenge is to think through the problem and

---

Example 1: Managing What and How

Now that we have a basic idea of what managers manage and how, it's time to meet some managers.

George is a branch manager of Growlers, a regional garage and car dealership business with ten branches. He directly manages a small team comprising the branch sales and service managers, a workshop supervisor and an office manager, and he has overall responsibility for the performance of the branch.

George's job is typical of lower level managerial jobs in that it combines managing with more hands-on activity. It is also quite varied. He covers for his bottom level managers when they are sick or on holiday, and likewise for two of the other branch managers. He authorizes the buying in of used cars and demonstrators, and sometimes negotiates sales' deals. He is the point of contact both for his own head office and for the marketing representatives of the car manufacturer represented by his branch, and is often off-site. His core role, though, is to manage the customer experience in the branch, as measured through post-sale and post-service surveys, and here he uses the information available, both formally and informally, to manage the people.

Melanie has built her career in nursing and is now a matron, working on the maternity wards of the Mid-County General Hospital. She manages a team of a dozen nurses in the delivery suites and the post-natal ward, being responsible both for their day-to-day work and for their professional development. This entails managing them directly but, since hospitals operate 24/7, and she can't be there all the time, she also has to manage through her lead nurses. Moreover, Melanie is also responsible for her ward area more generally: for ensuring cleanliness, infection control and so on. Since this relies on cleaners, maintenance staff, etc., who are not part of her own unit, she has to manage important parts of the wards through these people's own managers.

With links to patients, administrators and clinicians, matrons

come up with a solution, at which point the exercise comes to an end, as it must, because they are learning in a classroom and not in the real world. Real managers don't have the luxury of stopping at that point. They have to implement their solutions. Indeed they

are key figures in hospitals and, according to her job description, Melanie should be liaising with just about everybody in the hospital, from cleaners to doctors and from other matrons to facilities' managers – not to mention at least half a dozen people in the Foundation Trust, which governs another two hospitals, as well as hers. In theory, much of this can be done through sophisticated information systems, and much of Melanie's time is inevitably spent at the computer. But she knows from experience that not all the information gets fed in accurately, or makes sense, or gets looked at, and that face-to-face relationships are essential if the hospital as a whole is to do the best for its patients. So, in Melanie's case, managing people and managing information, managing through people and managing through information, managing her unit and managing the interfaces with other units, are all important and all fit tightly together.

As an example of a more senior manager, consider Ed, the managing director of a subsidiary division of Eagle Engineering, a general engineering and instrumentation company. Ed manages a manufacturing business with about 200 employees, including production facilities (a factory), product development, sales and accounts. HR, IT and other functions are managed from the parent company headquarters. Ed is responsible for a team of specialist managers covering the different parts of his business – a factory manager, a product development manager, a sales manager and so on – and on a day-to-day basis he manages largely through them, ensuring that their activities are properly informed and coordinated, and helping them to implement the strategies and policies that have been developed, with his help, by a team at the corporate headquarters. Both in people and information terms he is the gateway between the business and the wider corporation, and his management tasks reflect this. He reports in both directions: upwards, on the performance of the business and of his specialist managers; downwards, on strategy and incentive policies. He also meets regularly with union representatives, officiates at the factory Christmas party, and represents the firm in local business and community groups.

often have to start implementing before they've had much chance of working out what the solution will be. But they still have to think. Indeed good managers think rather a lot. This is not easily done.

It is almost impossible to find serious thinking time during the regular working day, which is filled with meetings, phone calls, texts, emails and routine tasks. So if thinking is to be done at all, it has to be in time specially set aside for it, which is rare, or away from work: in cars, trains or planes, in bed or in the bath. When managers do try to think, moreover, it's often not very productive, partly because they are too tired or their minds are too cluttered, and partly because, while they may have picked up some tools and techniques from business school, they've never learnt how to use them. We shall turn to tools and techniques in Chapters 4–7. Until then, the key message is simply that thinking matters. Even if they can't make the time for systematic analysis, or have to delegate that to someone else, good managers are always thinking about what they are doing, why they are doing it and what the consequences are.

A common caricature of managers is that they don't do anything themselves, but just tell other people what to do. If telling doesn't count as doing, then there's some truth in that. For what managers mainly do (having thought about it first) is 'tell' in one way or another, by speaking or writing. They tell people what the situation is, what needs to be done and why. They pass information to their staff, to their bosses and between themselves. They are, very largely, communicators. We must remember, however, that communication is as much about listening as it is about speaking, as much about reading as it is about writing. So the manager as speaker needs to be conscious of what the listener is hearing, which might be quite different from what was intended. And you can only tell people how to address a situation if you have first listened carefully while they tell you what the situation is, and how they are predisposed to act.

Managers don't only think, speak and listen; they also do things. But they do relatively little as managers, and when they do, the action itself is often less important than the messages it conveys. When managers act, their staff notice. Sometimes this is the whole point of the action. Managers demonstrate, through taking action themselves, how things should be done. Sometimes, however, managers act without properly thinking and undermine their own instructions and advice. Actions speak louder than words; so, however well-chosen your words, you need to make sure that your actions conform.

In summary, managers manage both what goes on inside their units and what happens at the boundaries. They manage both people and information, and they do it by thinking, speaking, listening and acting. With this basic structure in place, we can now look more closely at the different aspects of managing already identified: coping, controlling, administration, trouble-shooting, coaching, leading and accountability.

CHAPTER 2

Aspects of Managing

MANAGING AS COPING

Our first task on encountering any new situation is normally to cope. We may not use the word – we are more likely to think in terms of control, but it is control in the sense of being more or less in control, not in the sense of actively directing things. We begin by making sure we have control of ourselves: avoiding panic, not running away, not being frozen on the spot, like a rabbit in the headlights, unable to do anything. We then move on to achieving a stable footing, recognizing and coping with the environment, as well as with ourselves. Only once we have achieved that do we generally move towards active control and direction.

In this respect, management situations are much like any other situations. When you enter a management role or a new management role, when you take on new responsibilities or have them thrust upon you, your first challenge is to control yourself, to make sure that you are personally fit for action. With luck this will happen very quickly, but new responsibilities can be daunting. It is not unusual for first-time managers to begin by wandering around aimlessly, not knowing what they should be doing, or to keep doing their old jobs, clinging to the security those offer rather than facing up to the new challenge.

The challenge of coping in this most basic fashion can also arise from external events. You may face a crisis in your home life that is nothing to do with work but that takes you over, fills your thoughts and prevents you from functioning as you normally would. Or you may suffer from a disabling illness, such as depression or bipolar disorder, that can be kept under control most of the time, but that becomes a problem at times of stress, whether this arises from home or from work.

In circumstances such as these, you have a responsibility as a manager to limit any harm to your organization and especially to the people who work for you or depend directly on you. In the case of a crisis at home, you will quite rightly want to give priority to your family, and in the case of illness, it will be in everybody's interests for you to prioritize getting better. But if you fail even to cope at work, in the sense of keeping control of yourself, the demands on your colleagues will be massive. And even this basic level of coping is only sustainable for a very short period, as, while some things might get done, others certainly won't.

Fortunately, such circumstances are relatively rare, and assuming that you are more or less in control of yourself, the next step is to cope well, to be at least vaguely in control of yourself and your environment. We often talk of people in a new job 'finding their feet', by which we really mean finding their footholds: not just standing up but walking around, without falling down on the job.

This means getting the things done that need to be done: meeting your deadlines, communicating essential information, not letting people down and so on. It means not omitting to do anything essential, even if, in a more positive sense, you don't actually achieve very much. If you think of a single mother trying to 'manage' with several small children, the analogy is not a bad one.

Of course, as a manager you will want to go beyond just coping, even coping well, and the purpose of this book is to help you do that. But in practice, many managers don't. The Peter Principle, named after the humorous writer Laurence J. Peter, states that in a hierarchical bureaucracy, managers will be promoted to their level of incompetence. If you are good at a job, you get promoted and you keep getting promoted until you end up in a job that is beyond you, in which the most you can do is cope. The original intention may have been humorous, but sadly things do often work out that way. Few organizations have mechanisms whereby someone can be demoted, without great shame and blame, back to what they were best at. Cynics suggest that this is intentional. The Dilbert Principle, enunciated by another great humorist, the cartoonist Scott Adams, asserts that people are promoted to management because they are

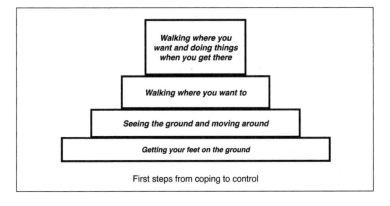

First steps from coping to control

incompetent: the higher they are promoted, the less damage they are capable of doing. This one really is a joke, however: bad managers can do immense harm and the more senior they are, the further that harm can spread.

Good managers will not just resign themselves to coping and no more. But nor will they sacrifice the basics in order to do something more, if that means doing it badly. The positive response to finding yourself at, or beyond, the limits of your competence is to extend your competence. Be honest with yourself; seek advice, seek mentoring and build slowly. If, as a reader of this book, you find your work is largely about coping, turn to the guidelines and address them, not wholesale but two or three at a time (most cluster naturally into pairs and triplets). Work on them steadily. Put them into practice. Monitor your efforts and get feedback from colleagues. And if you think a possible promotion may be a step too far, don't accept it, or accept it only with your reservations explicit and with arrangements in place for the support you will need.

MANAGING AS CONTROLLING

There are rather few managers in fiction, but one of the best known is actually called a controller: Sir Topham Hatt, the Fat Controller of the Thomas the Tank Engine series of children's books. In real life, Sir Topham's title would have been general manager, effectively the chief executive of a railway company or, after World War II, of a regional division of the nationalized British Railways.

As a manager, you will generally hope to do more than just be vaguely in control. You will hope to take control and actively direct the work of the unit for which you are responsible. The most obvious way of doing this is through the exercise of authority. In any hierarchical organization (and most organizations are hierarchical to at least some extent), people carry authority on account of their organizational status. There is a strong presumption that instructions coming from above will be followed, because that is the basis on which work is organized. Some people can also wield authority on the strength of their social status, their personal charisma or the respect in which they are held as individuals. The fictional Sir Topham embodies all of these: the chief executive of a hierarchical organization, a knight of the realm, a personally inspiring figure and a renowned engineer – which counted for a lot in a traditional railway company, even if it had nothing to do with the job in hand.

Authority is only part of the story, however, and it can be a liability, as well as an asset. It is only part of the story because it relates specifically to the managing of people and, as we have seen, you also need to be managing information. It can be a liability because it can lead to a manager's advice and instructions being followed far too readily. Being a knight of the realm or a good engineer is not necessarily relevant to running a business. Charismatic managers inspire fervent and unquestioning loyalty, which can be very dangerous if the manager should take a wrong turning, or turn that loyalty to personal rather than organizational advantage. One of the most common problems faced by corporate chief executives is that they can't even think aloud or float an idea without people taking it as an instruction and acting upon it.

Very rarely will good managers seek to control people in a strong sense. Some managers clearly do try to do this, either to gain personal power or through a strong conviction that they are right, or as a result of being carried away by the effects of charisma or status. Having experienced the power that control brings, they find that they rather like it. As a general rule, however, this kind of approach is neither ethical nor productive, and it does a lot of damage. In most organizations, the key to success is to get people to use their minds, to retain their critical faculties – not to question every instruction, which would be massively time and energy consuming, but to be able to question when necessary, and to apply the guidelines they receive from above in a thoughtful and intelligent way. Blind loyalty destroys this capacity.

There may, of course, be exceptional cases, such as in an extreme emergency, when you need to replicate the dynamics of an army in battle and secure people's unconditional obedience. But that is very rarely necessary and it can be very dangerous in an organization that is not set up in the appropriate way. Indeed, even in the armed forces, obedience rests as much on trust, and the demonstrated trustworthiness of the officers, as it does on discipline.

You should not normally seek to strongly control people as a manager, but you should seek to direct them: to point them in the right direction, to guide them and to instruct them, both in the sense of teaching them how to do things and, sometimes, in the narrower sense of giving them instructions. (Remember that giving instructions is not quite the same as giving orders. Orders are peremptory and rarely appropriate in management. Instructions come with opportunities for clarification and explanation.) You will also seek to exercise control through people: encouraging and enabling them to be proactive rather than reactive, to anticipate opportunities and challenges, and to turn new developments to advantage, and winning their support and enthusiasm for change.

All this involves information. Good managers don't control information either, in the sense of censoring it, but they do control information flows to make sure that the information needed is available, where it's needed and when. Whether you are reporting on the work of your unit to superiors and peers, or reporting on the direction of

---

Example 2: Coping and Controlling

Both Ed, the managing director, and George, the branch manager, are well established in their jobs and can reasonably be said to be in control. Their businesses may not be quite as successful as they or their superiors would ideally like, but run reasonably smoothly and perform pretty well. Melanie, the hospital matron, is also in reasonable control. In the administrative chaos of a national health system, things don't always go to plan. There are times when all she can do is cope. But she knows that she can cope, she's learnt how the system operates and she's worked out how to get things done when she needs to. What about some other managers?

As a primary school teacher and a mother herself, Polly knows a thing or two about coping and controlling, but she discovered more when she became headmistress of Portborough Primary, a large local authority governed primary school. It was a steep learning curve. She'd only been appointed deputy head, at another local school, a month before, and arrived to find her new school in turmoil after two heads had come and gone in quick succession, each trying to implement a raft of changes. It was tempting to plunge in herself and start putting things right, but was that really wise? Perhaps, she thought, the staff needed a bit of space and time to sort themselves out. And she certainly needed time to learn the job and get to know people, something that her predecessors had failed to do. She remembered the advice of one of her own former heads: don't try to run until you can (a) stand up and (b) see where you're going.

Polly took that advice and a year later it was beginning to pay dividends. It hadn't been an easy year, what with the local authority pressing for action and the teachers braced to resist it, and it would be going too far to say she was controlling things, but she was more or less in control. She was beginning to change things and she had a good idea, when she pulled any particular lever, how her varied staff were likely to react, how the parents were

the organization and other relevant developments to your unit, you will need, as a manager, to make sure that people have the information they need and, at the same time, that they are not swamped by information they don't need. A mass of redundant information is no more helpful than a lack of information, so you need to exercise

likely to react and, most important of all, what the impact would be on the children.

Rick's experience of the restaurant business has been of strongly autocratic, control-based cultures. Chefs ruled their kitchens with a rod of iron, threatening, insulting and quite often physically harming their staff. Maître d's tended to be more manipulating, controlling people emotionally rather than physically, but controlling them just the same. Owners and managers tried to control their chefs and maître d's, though they rarely succeeded. At the same time, the experience always seemed to be one of barely coping. Service was always on a knife edge, disaster always just around the corner.

Having worked his way up through this system, Rick is now himself manager of a city restaurant and bar/nightclub, owned by a successful investment banker, and he is trying to come to grips with the challenge it presents. The element of coping seems inescapable. With the high staff turnover characteristic of the sector, fickle customers and rapidly changing fashions, he can never feel completely in control. And with the passions aroused in pursuit of culinary excellence he is always having to steady the ship. The control culture, too, seems hard to avoid. His chef seeks control of the kitchen and the owner, used to doing whatever he wants, seeks control over him. But, he thinks to himself, it's surely not controlling people that matters. Because the margins between success and failure are so small, control certainly does matter, but what the chef really wants to control is not his staff, but the quality of the food they serve up. And what the owner really wants to control is not him, Rick, but the quality of the overall customer experience (and, of course, the quantity of the profits). To build on these thoughts he's been introducing feedback and review sessions, and agreeing objectives and performance levels with the staff, and trying to achieve control that way. The chef still screams at the sous-chefs, but now he does it just to remind them when they start losing the plot, not to frighten the life out of them.

control over what is actively communicated and what is just made available for reference.

Managers also control through information. Indeed, for many managers this is a large part of the job. Most obviously, you draw up budgets, which control the allocation of resources. You also analyse both the environment – customer needs, competitor offerings, etc. – and your available skills and resources, so as to draw up plans for the future. You set targets, monitor and measure performance against them, carry out appraisals and assessments, and give feedback. Some of this imposes controls on the work of your unit. Some of it serves more loosely to keep control of situations as they evolve.

MANAGING AS ADMINISTRATION

The spectrum of activities from coping through to controlling is reflected in all the different dimensions of managing. A manager who is barely coping is unlikely to (and certainly shouldn't) be leading, coaching or even trouble-shooting. Managers who are coping well, but not getting beyond that, may be able to do some trouble-shooting and coaching. Indeed, they may have been very proficient at a more junior level and able to offer some very valuable coaching. But they are in no position to coach people towards taking the kind of position they hold themselves, or to exercise effective leadership. Leadership requires the ability to take control, albeit often in quite subtle ways, and to enable others to take control.

Because it is seen as relatively straightforward and unchallenging, routine administration is very much the poor relation among management tasks. Many managers complain about how tedious it is, how much time it takes up, and how much better that time could be used doing something more interesting and more productive. They see it, in short, as a waste of time. In consequence, it is often neglected or done in only a perfunctory way.

This is a big mistake. The whole point of organizations is that they organize work, but this doesn't happen by itself. Organization depends on operating systems of various kinds, and these have to be operated and maintained. It is true that bureaucracy has an in-built tendency to expand. In any bureaucratic organization at any one time there are almost certainly more reports to be written and read, and more committees to be attended, than would be ideal. And both the reports and the meetings are quite probably longer than would be ideal. But they are mostly there for good reasons. They are like cogs in a machine, and if one of them is neglected and fails, the whole machine breaks down.

In less bureaucratic organizations, routine administration may take different forms, with informal meetings instead of formal committees, less formal reports and much less rigid timetables. But the work of keeping things going smoothly and effectively still has to be done. Resources have to be allocated. Budgets have to be set and reviewed. Tasks have to be delegated. Performance measures have to be devised and performance has to be monitored and assessed. Recommendations have to be reviewed. Actions have to be formally signed off, both to ensure clarity and to provide legal protection. Risk assessments have to be carried out, and health and safety assured. Staff have to be appraised. Complaints have to be reviewed. Grievances have to be addressed. In any but the smallest organizations, appointments, promotions, staff reviews and disciplinary matters will require the involvement of several managers, including people from outside the unit, both to ensure fairness and to achieve better decisions.

To neglect these activities, as some managers do, is not only to let down the organization, which is bad enough, but also to let down the individuals whose well-being depends on them, which is arguably worse. Most organizations can cope if a small percentage of their managers are less than diligent on the administrative front. But if someone fails to get promotion who deserves it, gets no response to be being bullied, is badly injured because no-one could be troubled to make sure that heavy objects were not stored on high, open shelves, gets a poor assessment because they weren't given the resources to do their job probably, or just struggles because of a thoughtless task allocation or performance measure – these things really matter. That person could have been you, and as a good manager you will remember that and take care that your routine administration is done conscientiously.

If you do this, moreover, you will also reap personal benefits. The writer G. K. Chesterton once remarked, in connection with a hat being blown off and carried away by the wind, that an inconvenience is only an adventure wrongly considered. Routine administration is rarely an adventure, but if approached in the right spirit, and not just as an inconvenience, it can be very satisfying. It can be very satisfying to be the manager of an effective and happy team, and to know that people's efforts and abilities are properly recognized and rewarded, that their well-being is properly looked after. It can be very satisfying to know that you have completed things satisfactorily. And there is much to be said for a working life that combines difficult challenges with elements of routine. If you treat routine administration as an inconvenience and don't do it properly, its presence will just add to your stress levels. If you value it for what it is and give it your full attention, it can not only be a welcome distraction from more stressful and more demanding tasks, but can help you to focus much more clearly on these.

MANAGING AS TROUBLE-SHOOTING

The British Prime Minister Harold Macmillan, when asked by a journalist what was most likely to throw governments off course, is reputed to have answered, 'Events, dear boy, events'. By which he meant the unexpected, unforeseen and often unforeseeable: suddenly erupting foreign wars or political crises, speculative pressures on the currency, security threats, the death or illness of key figures, political scandals, failed harvests or unusually severe winters.

'Events' are a fact of life in any management context, not just in government, and we can distinguish very crudely between two kinds. First, there are the big one-off events that totally disrupt operations and have to be dealt with. A shop or restaurant is gutted by fire. A dock strike, terrorist attack or extreme weather event prevents the delivery of crucial supplies. A major customer is bankrupted. A project goes disastrously over-budget. A key person falls ill or has an accident at a critical point of a project. Hidden emotions rise to the service under pressure and leave a team dysfunctional. Somebody makes a mistake or omits to do something that is only discovered when it's too late to rectify.

Second, there are the smaller but more persistent events that constitute what we usually call 'trouble'. There may be repeated disruptions of supplies or a series of customer complaints. There might be a series of small-scale industrial actions, of grievances, disciplinary cases or personal spats. Deadlines might be repeatedly missed or budgets repeatedly exceeded. Or there might be recurrent mistakes, none serious enough to constitute a major event in itself but indicative, taken together, of a significant underlying problem.

What both types of event have in common is that they can only be dealt with through managerial action. Whether the trouble is caused by something going wrong in the unit for which you are responsible or by something quite outside your control, you have as a manager, or as part of a managerial team, to deal with it. If it's within your power to fix something, you fix it. If it's not, you work with your colleagues to find a way around it.

Of the two types of event, the first may seem the most challenging and disruptive but it is often the easier to deal with, if only because it has to be dealt with. There is a crisis. You have to respond. The show must go on. As a manager – or, if the problem goes beyond your unit, as a group of managers – you have the formal authority, you have access to the information, you have the interpersonal networks and people will expect you to use them. So you do what managers do. You gather, share and analyse information. You think through the problem. You make a decision on how to deal with it or, at least to start off with, on how to begin dealing with it. And you use your interpersonal and communications skills, your networks and, where appropriate, your technical skills, to get it implemented.

One of the characteristics of trouble-shooting in response to one-off events is that it is when you are most likely, as a manager, to take direct action – to do a job yourself that you would normally delegate to others. If you are in danger of losing a major customer, for example, it might well be that with your past experience, knowledge and personal relationships, you can recover the situation in a way that no-one else could. Or if, in a professional or craft context, someone has made a bad mistake or been taken ill at a critical stage of a project, you may well need to roll up your sleeves and finish the job yourself if it is to be done satisfactorily. Wherever possible you will also use this as an opportunity to teach others, remembering that you are a manager, but sometimes the crisis is such that you just have to resolve it and everything else goes by the board.

The second type of event is much more difficult, for two closely connected reasons. First, if people are not doing things properly or correctly, for whatever reason, on a modest but persistent basis, it is not a good idea to just step in and do them yourselves. This may be the easiest route in the short term, but it doesn't address the underlying problem. Second, if no individual event prompts a crisis, there is no imperative to act. It is always possible to let things ride, to hope that they will right themselves, to hope that things won't blow up on your watch or simply, given how busy you are, to defer action until the next time... and the next, and the next. But this is an even worse idea than doing the job yourself. It doesn't address the short-term problem or the underlying one. It just allows things to deteriorate, so that what started out as a problem that could have been solved, relatively easily, becomes a persistent trouble that just gets harder and harder to solve the longer it persists – until at some point it erupts as a crisis that is by then far too deep-seated to be resolved without massive pain and disruption.

The temptation to deal with troubles by either doing the job your-self or putting off addressing the problem is probably most danger-ous when the troubles arise from mistakes. Reading most of what's written on management you'd think that no-one ever made mistakes but, of course, they do – all the time. We all do. And responding to mistakes is one of the most important parts of managing as trouble-shooting.

Some mistakes are just accidental one-offs, temporary aberra-tions. If they occur in your unit you should note them, mention them (or admit to them, if they are yours) and move on. Some mistakes are part of the learning process. As people stretch their competence and learn new skills, they don't always get it right first time, and if they did, they probably wouldn't be stretching them-selves far enough. The important thing here is that the mistakes are learnt from, that you treat them, as a manager, constructively, as opportunities not as failings. Some mistakes are indicative that the person isn't up to the job and isn't learning, and here some judge-ments need to be made. Can the situation be remedied by training and development, or is there a fundamental problem of competency that needs to be addressed through the appropriate procedures, which may result in the person moving to a less demanding role or leaving the organization altogether? Sometimes there may be more than just incompetence but an element of wilful neglect that needs to be dealt with through disciplinary procedures. And sometimes mistakes are a sign of problems in someone's personal life – stresses, illness, preoccupations, emotional entanglements – that may call for support and counselling, for help through a difficult period.

If you think of the implications these judgements have not only for the work of the unit, but also for the people concerned, it quickly becomes apparent how important it is for the manager to get them right.

MANAGING AS COACHING

In French and Spanish, the word 'manager' had, until very recently, stuck at an earlier stage of its evolution than in English and was largely reserved for the manager of a sports' team or individual, what the Americans would call a coach. (In American terminol-ogy, the 'manager' in this context would be a commercial agent, handling the business affairs, not someone responsible for sporting performance.) In British football (both soccer and rugby), the terms 'manager' and 'coach' are often interchangeable, and this reflects the fact that coaching is an important part of management. The manager of a group or team, in the sense of someone who is responsible for their work, is also – or should also be – a coach.

Coaching takes place on various levels. The primary objective is generally to help people to improve their performance in whatever activities their jobs require. As a manager, you will be in a similar position here to a tennis coach working with a tennis player, and you will use the same kinds of techniques and approaches. You will observe someone in action and give them constructive feedback on things they could do better, drawing on a mixture of established knowledge and your own personal experience. Sometimes you will demonstrate how a task should be done: how to treat customers, how to respond to complaints or how to execute a particular skill, whether phrasing a legal sentence, replacing a car component, plastering into a corner or operating a machine. Sometimes you will recommend that someone practises a particular procedure or takes a particular training course.

At low skill levels, this kind of coaching might be quite basic, and as much to do with supplementing someone's general education or changing their habits as with developing their job-specific skills. They might need to enlarge their vocabulary, for example, or just to smile more. This doesn't make it any less important or any less a part of your job as a manager. A good manager doesn't just accept that Jack can't count properly or isn't sociable, but recognizes that those are things that might, with help, be worked on and improved.

At higher levels, and especially when you are coaching people who are already managers, the skills needed might again be generic, so that coaching someone involves acting as a sounding board or devil's advocate, rather than as an advisor.

Sometimes coaching involves more than just someone's work performance, especially if they have the potential to advance beyond their current job. Almost any teacher, at any level and in any context, is engaged in two simultaneous tasks. One is to teach something specific – a subject, a syllabus. The other is to help people grow – to open their minds, stretch their horizons, build their confidence and so on – and, in the process, to give them a leg up as they climb and catch them if they fall. Now many teachers are not consciously aware, or not strongly aware, of this second task. It is all they can do to convey the information or, in a school context, to keep control of the class. Good teachers are very aware of it, however, and so are good coaches and good managers. Technical coaching can get people so far, but there comes a point, even in quite technical contexts, where what someone brings to the task as a person is what makes the difference. And developing someone's specific work skills will do no good at all if, in the process, the pressures of work or of home or of ambition pull them apart.

One further aspect of coaching that should be mentioned here is the coaching of work teams. A manager, like a football coach, is typically concerned both with individuals and with a team, and enhancing the performance of the individuals is only part of the coaching task. The individuals also have to be coached to work effectively together, which involves making them aware of their own and others' contributions, and how these fit together; of their own and others' weaknesses, and what can be done as a team to mitigate the effects of these. Just as in football the defence have to hold a line, the strikers sometimes have to fall back and help defend, and the players generally have to be aware of each others' positions and of the opportunities and gaps created, so organizational teams have to interact effectively, adjust as a team to changing circumstances, and support and cover for each other. Given their inevitable focus on their own particular tasks, this often requires careful coaching.

MANAGING AS LEADING

In both trouble-shooting and coaching, managing takes on an element of leadership. There are all sorts of definitions of leadership, ranging from the personality traits required of a leader to the processes by which people lead. There are also, corresponding to these, all sorts of distinctions made between leadership and management. So, one author distinguishes between managing as doing things right and leading as doing the right things. Another distinguishes between managing an organization in steady state and leading a change in the organization. Others characterize leadership in terms of the ability to transform people's inner lives, while managers just affect their outward behaviours. The simplest definition of leading, however, is just 'being followed', and from this perspective it is part and parcel of managing. The manager's challenge is to be make sure that you are followed, as and when appropriate, but also that you are not followed inappropriately, that you don't unintentionally lead people astray.

One classic account of leadership in a management context identified three key tasks: establishing a direction, aligning people in that direction, and motivating and inspiring them to keep to the path set, despite the obstacles that will inevitably arise. The context here was the management of change in large bureaucratic organizations, which are notoriously resistant to change, but the recipe can be adapted to a more general management context.

Change poses a problem for any organization, large or small. People acquire habits and old habits die hard. People become comfortable with ways of doing things and it's hard to break out of your comfort zone. Organizations develop characteristic cultures – values and norms, ways of doing things, ways of thinking. These are typically rooted in what worked well in the past and may well be unsuited to present challenges, but they are often deeply embedded in the language, practices, routines and even the physical artefacts of the organization, and they can be immensely hard to shift.

As a manager, you may need to initiate change, in your own business, for example, or as a chief executive. Or you may need to implement changes imposed on you by your superiors, or by regulators and other external agencies. In such cases it is often not enough just to put new arrangements in place. You also have to win people over to the new way of doing things, communicating the change in direction required and the reasons for it, aligning people to follow you in that direction, inspiring and motivating them to break out of their old habits and to overcome the resistance that change inevitably brings. Any new departure introduces uncertainty and runs the risks both of a lack of clarity in direction and of a reversion to the old ways.

Sometimes, you will need much the same leadership skills, even though there is no significant change required. You may need a push for performance in response to the moves of a competitor, or just to demonstrate the value of your unit in response to political machinations elsewhere in the organization. You may just need to hold a team together in the face of strong individual personalities or conflicting interests. Whereas old-fashioned bureaucracies face the problem that people conform too tightly to established ways of doing things, much more loosely structured, contemporary organizations often face the opposite problem. Reward structures based on individual performance and the pursuit of self-interest can encourage staff ambitious to earn more and get ahead to neglect the interests of their team or unit, and focus much more on securing their next job than on carrying out their current one. Creative entrepreneurial cultures can result in people going off in all sorts of different directions, leaving the unit as a whole with no direction at all. Think of people as magnetic iron filings and a leader as someone exerting a magnetic attraction to pull them all into line.

One problem, of course, is that the direction has to be the right direction. There's no point pulling people along with you if you are going the wrong way yourself. And if you're able to exert a magnetic attraction on people, whether through the force of your personality or through the position you hold, it might act when you don't want

---

Example 3: Facets of Managing

All the managers we have introduced so far have jobs that combine administration, trouble-shooting, coaching and leadership. This is most obvious, ironically, with the two who aren't called 'managers', though that's certainly what they are. Both Melanie, the matron, and Polly, the head teacher, working in the context of public sector bureaucracies, are plagued by administration, filling forms and generating paper trails to show (though they don't actually show) that the endless policies and procedures to which they are subject are being followed. Responsible for patients and small children, they are constantly trouble-shooting in response to accidents and emergencies. In caring professions they are expected to pass on their accumulated knowledge and experience to others. And in settings where so much depends on the culture of the unit and the attitudes of staff, they have to be leaders too.

George, the garage manager, would be surprised to hear himself called a leader. He's not especially charismatic, he's never been one of those who just had to be captain of the team, and the branch manager of a car dealership on the outskirts of Wolverhampton isn't something he'd ever have thought of as a leadership role. But he knows that the way to deliver a positive customer experience is for everyone to pull together and to be, and to come across as, a team, and he works hard at that. Acting on the customer feedback he finds himself doing a fair bit of coaching, and he has his load of administration, mainly to do with staff appraisals, recruitment and promotion and approvals of one kind and another. Trouble-shooting is mainly restricted to minor incidents in the workshop or on-road testing, but there was also that time when there was a major fire at another branch, the manager there couldn't cope, and he had to step in and sort things out.

Rick, the restaurant manager, on the other hand, seems to

it to. People might follow blindly when you want them to think for themselves, or copy what you do instead of doing what you ask. What you want as a manager, and what your employers will want you to have as a manager, is respect, not adoration. And respect – unlike charisma or even status – has to be continuously earned.

---

spend much of his time trouble-shooting: it's the nature of the business. But it would be much worse if he wasn't also on top of the administration, especially in respect of the health and safety and other regulations that a restaurant cannot afford to take lightly. Leading the team is probably harder for him than it is for George, but even more critical, since one person singing out of tune can wreck the customer experience. And coaching is part of that. He actually hopes that some of his staff will go on to manage restaurants themselves, and does what he can to help them learn. In this industry he will lose them sometime anyway, and by coaching, he can both keep them a bit longer and build a reputation for the restaurant as a place where the most talented youngsters want to work.

Ed also has his fair share of trouble-shooting. If there are problems on the factory floor, the headquarters HR people deal with any negotiations, but he has to deal with the practical consequences of strike action, like missed deadlines and unfulfilled orders. A more persistent 'trouble' is called Derek, a section head, who is neither incompetent nor disobedient but just does things his own way, which is never quite what is wanted.

Derek is un-coachable, but Ed does try and coach his other section heads, and he also tries to identify potential talent lower down the organization and to set in place systems to support, monitor and develop the people concerned. He is also seen by his employees as a leader, not because he shouts 'leader' – the culture of the organization has been in place a long time and the changes he's made have been relatively modest – but because people expect the managing director to be a leader, and he doesn't let them down. When people need a figurehead or a representative, he gives them one. When they need guidance or need an answer or need to understand changes coming down from the corporate centre, he gives them those. He doesn't set out to lead but, like all successful managers, he fills a leadership role.

MANAGEMENT AND ACCOUNTABILITY

The last of the dimensions of managing we shall cover in this part of the book is not so much something managers do, as something they are. Managers are accountable, not only for the work they do themselves but also for the work done by the people they manage, both individually and as a group. To be accountable for something means that you can be required to give an account of it and be held to that account. In particular, if something goes wrong – whether it is a question of performance targets being missed or of ethical or regulatory failings – you can be required to give an explanation of what went wrong and why, and judged on that explanation.

To see how this works, we can consider three familiar cases of accountability. First, a football team performs poorly or fails to meet the expectations of the club owner or, if it's a national team, of the supporters and general public. Here the team manager (or coach) is typically held to account and may well find his contract terminated, even if the expectations were quite unrealistic, given the resources at his disposal.

Second, a school inspection reveals poor results in some subject, or a problem with some student records, staff behaviour or health and safety procedures. Here the person with managerial responsibility, usually the school head, is held to account, even though the problem may be attributable to just one member of staff.

Third, a large business corporation posts results that are considered by press and shareholders to be disappointing. Here, managers may be held to account and at risk of termination at a number of different levels: business unit managers, divisional managers, marketing managers and so on, up to, and including, the chief executive.

Accountability serves various functions. For the owner-manager of a small business, it is a simple fact of life. If you own a firm of builders and one of your plumbers fits something badly, it is your reputation that will suffer. In a professional firm, it is a way of safeguarding professional standards. The national and international codes of conduct governing the accounting profession stipulate that all work carried out must be done under the supervision of a named, qualified accountant and, even if the supervision is in practice minimal (a name on a piece of paper), that person is fully accountable for it. In the case of a school, where the present and future lives of children are at stake, it is crucial that nothing should fall between the gaps of different people's responsibilities, and this is achieved by having one person accountable for the whole operation.

In other cases, however, accountability may have less to do with assuring standards and more to do with allocating blame. In the case of football managers, where turnover is ridiculously high, taking the blame is evidently part and parcel of the job. Much the same is true of the chief executives of large corporations, who know that 'the buck stops here', and that they are more likely to be terminated or to 'step down by mutual agreement' than to retire in post or leave of their own accord.

Inside large organizations, where accountability sits at multiple levels of management, we see complex blame games being played out. When things go wrong, or don't go as well as hoped, more senior managers seek to exonerate themselves by laying the blame on lower levels. Perhaps the managers beneath them were appointed by a predecessor and not of their choosing. Perhaps, though 'everyone agreed' that the junior managers had shown promise, it was now clear that they were not up to the challenge and needed to be moved on. Junior managers, similarly, try to clear themselves: it was the strategy or direction set by their superiors that was at fault, not their implementation of it.

The way these issues typically get resolved is by a combination of rational analysis, personal negotiation and organizational politics. The result is not always fair and the process can be very difficult for the managers involved. There is always a temptation to join in the game when blame is being thrown around. And it is all too easy to respond to criticism either by being overly defensive or by turning aggressively on your critics. None of these are advisable.

The root of the problem, and what turns accountability from a constructive force to a destructive one, is the deeply felt need many people have – and have always had – to attribute blame. When things go wrong, it is very often a result of multiple, interconnected issues, some of which can be traced to individuals, some to the interactions between individuals, some to embedded features of the organization or society and some to events quite outside anybody's control. No one person is properly speaking to blame, but we need to find someone, some scapegoat, we can blame. And if an inquiry of some kind concludes that there isn't one, we condemn it as a whitewash or cover-up.

Of course, some inquiries are whitewashes and cover-ups, as powerful people find ways to protect themselves or people simply avoid facing up to the problems that an organization has. It is both easy and dangerous to slide from (rightly) not wishing to blame people to (wrongly) not holding them accountable. But the more common problem for managers is the opposite slide, from (rightly) holding people accountable to (wrongly) blaming them, and this slide is so familiar that we often assume it's happening even when it isn't. So we misinterpret what are intended as genuine, if critical, questions as if they were imputations of blame, and respond by trying to defend ourselves instead of answering the questions. Good managers learn to avoid this trap and, generally, to avoid getting into questions of blame. The important thing is always to work out what happened and why, and to learn how things can be done better.

Example 4: Accountability

In practice, most managers have multiple accountabilities. Melanie, for example, is formally accountable to her boss's boss in the Foundation Trust, the director of nursing, but she sees herself above all as accountable to the patients who come through her wards, to the mothers and babies, and to their partners and families. Similarly, Polly is formally accountable to the governors of the school, a mixture of parent, teacher, community and local authority representatives, and through them to the local authority. She is also held to account by the regulator, OFSTED, and is often held to be accountable to the children's parents. But she sees herself as accountable, in addition, to a kind of fictional guardian of the children's interests, which are never quite represented by governors, regulators or parents.

Both Melanie and Polly also hold themselves accountable to their own staff, whose lives depend, to some extent, on how well they manage; this is generally true of good managers. George, Rick and Ed all feel something of the same. In other respects, though, their accountabilities are much more straightforward: George and Ed to their bosses and through them to the owners and shareholders of the businesses, and Rick to the restaurant owner.

CHAPTER 3

Fifty Guidelines for Effective Managing

1 THE FIRST REQUIREMENT: INTEGRITY AND HUMANITY

The first recorded management consultant was the Ancient Chinese sage, Confucius, who lived over 2,500 years ago and built his career mentoring candidates for Imperial Office. In some ways the advice he gave was peculiar to the culture and period, but much of it applies remarkably well to the challenges of modern management.

A key feature of Confucius's advice was that it combined the ethical with the pragmatic. His core value was *rèn* (also transcribed as *rvn* or *jen*), which corresponded to being a complete person: a combination of what we would call integrity and humanity or human-heartedness. At one level this signified an ideal that might rarely or never be achieved. A person with *rèn* would not only be completely honest, trustworthy, just, magnanimous, faithful, kind, benevolent, compassionate and so on, but would be unable to be anything other than these. At another, more realistic, level it signified a base on which to build. A person without *rèn*, he suggested, a person without integrity or humanity, could achieve nothing.

The ethical aspect of integrity and humanity is easy to see – they are qualities we all value and admire. But in thinking about managing, the more practical aspect is also important.

Integrity is something that is hard to define but easy to recognize. We can sense if people are fundamentally honest, if they mean what they say, if they are true to themselves, if their actions are generally consistent with their words. All these are indicators of integrity. And we can sense too if they are two-faced, devious, hypocritical or corruptible, all indicators of a lack of integrity. If, as a manager, you maintain your integrity, people will recognize that and respect you for it. The people who work for you will be inclined to do what you ask, and the people you work for will be inclined to recognize your achievements and support you if things go wrong. If you lack integrity, people will recognize that too. You may get away with it in the short run, and even achieve some quick successes, albeit at other people's expense, but in the longer run you will lose people's respect and their support. And once you lose it, you may never regain it.

Integrity is always a work in progress and, for the person concerned, a matter of degree. We are all tempted sometimes to slip into saving face, or easy fibs, or false assurances, and we have to work hard not to succumb. Anyone with a good measure of integrity would be the first to admit that they don't have complete integrity, that they fall short of their own ideals. To the observer, however, integrity is more a matter of black and white. People will assume that you either have it or don't have it, they will judge you on your failures not your successes, and one failure will often be enough to mark you for good.

In some fields, this poses an almost impossible challenge. In representative politics, for example, it is almost possible to get elected without promising some things you won't be able to deliver. Hypocrisy goes with the territory and the higher politicians rise, the more certain they are to be condemned as lacking integrity, quite irrespective of the fact that many of them actually have considerable integrity. Management, fortunately, is more straightforward. Maintain your integrity as best you can and it is likely to be recognized.

Humanity or human-heartedness is rather less obvious as a fundamental requirement of a manager. We recognize its value in a person, of course, but a feeling persists that it's not always appropriate to the technical task of managing. Isn't there a danger in a manager being too kind? Can't we manage more efficiently without it?

No, we can't! It helps if managers don't get too emotional, but a fundamental kindness and concern for other people – that sense of humanity that Christians call love or Buddhists loving-kindness – is the bedrock of any kind of management. You will even find it in the best generals who, for all their cool and calculated strategies, will never send soldiers into battle without a deep awareness of what they are doing in human terms. The ethical principle – always treat people as people and not just as a means to an end – works also as a practical principle. Recognize the value in people and you will find the value in people. Treat people properly and, by and large, they will behave properly.

2 IF YOU WANT TO BE LISTENED TO (AND YOU DO), FIRST EARN PEOPLE'S RESPECT

We have seen that one of the most important things you do as a manager is communicate, through speech and writing, with the people who work for you, the people you work for and work with, and other relevant stakeholders. You explain what has happened and what's going to happen. You tell people what to do and why. It is pretty obvious that you can only do this effectively if people listen to you, and listen carefully and attentively. But why should they listen?

You might hope that people will listen to you simply because you have something to say that they either want to know, should want to know or need to know, to do their own jobs properly. But it doesn't always work like that. They may think that they know better than you, that your views are not worth listening to or that the matter is just not important enough to warrant their attention. They may not want to be told what to do, if they think they might not want to do it or prefer to keep on doing whatever they are doing now. They may think they know what you are going to say and not be bothered to check if they're right.

There are basically three reasons why people may listen carefully to you when they might otherwise be inclined not to. All will be familiar from your schooldays, when your teachers faced a similar problem.

- One is fear: the fear that they might in some way be tested on what is being said and punished or denied something if they get the answers wrong.
- The second is personal attachment: the kind of love or adoration that makes people hang on someone's every word.
- The third is respect: the respect for someone that inclines people both to do them the courtesy of listening and to assume that they will have something useful to say.

There is no place in management for making people afraid, any more than there is in education. It is inconsistent with basic humanity. There is no place for adoration either. Fortunately, most adult workers have grown out of childhood crushes, so it is very rare, but when it does happen, it is just disruptive: difficult for the managers to handle, a distraction for the people drawn to them and a nuisance for those people's colleagues. So that leaves respect.

Why, then, might people respect you? Because, and only because, you have earned their respect. Some people are naturally respectful and will actively look for qualities in you that they can respect. But these people are probably a small minority, and even with them you will have to do your bit. With most people you will have to work much harder.

The best way of earning and holding people's respect in the longer term is by demonstrating the qualities of integrity and humanity we have just discussed. But this can take time and it may not be enough on its own. We can highly respect someone as a person and still judge them to be lacking in competence at their job, for example. So respect has to be earned in other ways too and, in particular, through achievement.

It can be tremendously helpful, as a manager, if you have a record of achievement, either in the jobs of the people you manage, or in the job you are doing, or in something than can be closely related to these. In some cases, this comes ready made. The people who manage professional firms, groups of scientists or the top universities are generally people who have excelled in the areas they are now managing. The same is often true of people who set up their own businesses in a skilled trade, of industrial supervisors, army NCOs and others who have worked their way up through the ranks. Here there is a basis for respect, a kind of reservoir on which you can draw, while learning to master the new job.

In other cases, you may come into a unit or organization with a track record in a similar job to that you are now doing, or just in some area that is valued by the organization, even if it is not obviously relevant: a distinguished sporting or military record, for example. Again this can buy you time. In many cases, however, you will have no such advantages and then you will have to work hard on two fronts simultaneously: demonstrating your competence at the job in hand, and demonstrating that you understand, appreciate, and would be both able and willing to take on the jobs your staff are doing, and to do at least some of them well.

One other thing that can quickly earn you a measure of respect, apart from competence and achievement, is your general bearing and behaviour. Some managers try to be 'one of the lads' but, while this can help bond a team together, it should be reserved for special occasions. On a day-to-day basis, you will earn people's respect by being dignified (but not aloof), friendly (but not too familiar), courteous and polite, smartly turned out (within the culture of the organization), calm, purposive and efficient; by acknowledging people, expressing an interest in them, and remembering their names, duties and a few things about them. Little things, but they matter to people.

3 RESPECT EVERYONE, HOWEVER LOWLY OR INCOMPETENT

The flip side of earning other people's respect is to respect other people – and to find ways of respecting them, even if their achievements seem to you quite minimal.

Many of us are not naturally respectful, so this can be quite a challenge, especially where people strike us as lazy or incompetent, as lacking self-respect, as weak-willed or as not pulling their weight. The first question to ask, therefore, is why should we respect such people?

Once again the answer combines ethical and practical considerations. From an ethical perspective, all human beings are worthy of our respect. The Universal Declaration of Human Rights, for example, begins by invoking the 'inherent dignity... of all members of the human family', and this theme is reflected in the teachings of all the major religions and all the major ethical philosophies. To deny it is to deny our own humanity.

From a more practical point of view, a failure to respect people carries at least four risks. There is the risk, first of all, of losing touch with our humanity. If we start by treating some people as unworthy of our personal respect, it is a small step to seeing classes of people as unworthy of anyone's respect, and so to the abuses of slavery and oppression – or at least to institutionally embodied prejudice, which is not a recipe for good management.

A second risk is that if we fail to respect them, we will lose their respect for us. This is easy to discount. If you see yourself as significantly 'better' than someone else – more capable, more talented, more successful – you might consider it quite natural that they should respect you and not the other way around. But respect doesn't work like that. Just as people who are deprived of love are often incapable of loving, people who feel they are not respected lose the capacity for respecting others. Respect just ceases to have any place in their lives.

A third risk is that by injuring their self-respect we disable them and make them even less capable than they were before. Some measure of self-respect is essential to the formation of character, to a basic notion of who we are. For anyone with limited capability, whether through disability, disadvantage, a lack of talent or a lack of will-power, this grounding of self-respect can be very fragile. It is embodied in the story they tell about themselves, and it relies on someone taking that story seriously. If people who matter, such as their managers, don't take it seriously, then one of two things happens: either those people cease to matter to them, and lose their respect, or else the story itself falls apart and with it their control over their lives.

The fourth risk is that if we fail to respect people, we will fail to listen to them. If you don't listen to somebody, you won't be able to recognize and make use of what they can contribute – and everybody can contribute something. And you won't notice if something goes seriously wrong.

For all these reasons it is important to find some way of respecting everybody who works for you, however lowly, unimportant, lazy or incompetent they may appear. So how do you go about it?

The first thing to remember is that they are doing a job. They are earning a living. And from where they started out or from where

---

Example 5: Respect

Earning people's respect is always going to be easier for some managers than for others, and easier in some contexts than others. Both Ed, the engineering company managing director, and Melanie, the hospital matron, brought to their jobs the skills and experience needed, and track records of achievement in the areas they were now overseeing. Gaining people's respect was relatively straightforward. George, the garage branch manager, earned his respect the hard way, by doing his job well, always going the extra mile and always respecting others. Working in a much smaller organization, people also got to know him quite well personally, to respect him as a person and to carry that respect into the workplace.

Polly, the headmistress, had to work even harder. She was younger than many of her teaching staff and unknown to them, and her two predecessors had created a culture of suspicion in which respect was not easily granted. She had to earn respect through her professionalism, dedication to the school and sound judgement, and by showing respect to her colleagues. In Rick, the restaurant manager's world, things were a bit different. In an industry where people were used to being ordered around and badly treated, respect for managers was rare and he could, to some extent, manage without it. What he couldn't do that way was get people to work together for the business as a whole, compromise and adapt when necessary, and give their best. Just

they were left by life's vicissitudes, that might in itself be a considerable achievement. People cannot choose their genes or their parents and upbringing, and it is always worth remembering that much of what we pride ourselves on, whether it be our talents, our values or our propensity to hard work, was probably either inherited or impressed on us by others, and none of our own doing at all.

Look hard for what people value, take pride in or are able to do well. Understand why they value or take pride in it, or are able to do it better than other things. Learn to see the world as they see it, as you would if they were characters in a sympathetic novel or film. There will always be something, somewhere, that you can empathize with and on the basis of which you can build respect. There may even be something they can teach you.

---

as Polly had to show people through her actions that she was a different kind of head from those they had recently experienced, Rick had to show people that he was a different kind of manager – and that by creating an environment of mutual respect, everyone could benefit.

Respecting other people is also more challenging for some managers than others. Polly and Melanie have no difficulty respecting their professional staff: they have been there too. But they also have to listen to, and respect, the cleaners and the various unqualified assistants without whom their wards and school would struggle. Often it is these people, outside and unconstrained by the core culture of the unit, who notice when something is wrong or who bring ideas for improvement.

Ed knows that treating the workers with respect as individuals is not only morally right but also makes for easier relationships with the trade unions and a more productive and less stressful working environment. George treats his branch rather like an extended family. People have their faults and their idiosyncrasies, but he can also see their strengths, and since most of them are there for the long term, it makes sense to build a reservoir of mutual respect that will get them through any arguments or difficulties. For Rick it is mainly a question of getting the best out of people. By giving people his respect, he gives them some pride in their jobs, however humble, and encourages them to do better.

4 IF YOU WANT TO BE TRUSTED (AND YOU DO), ALWAYS BE TRUSTWORTHY

Just as people will only listen to you if they respect you, they will only act as you wish if they trust you. And just as you have to earn their respect, so you have to earn their trust. The only way you can do that is by being trustworthy: by delivering on your promises and not promising what you can't deliver; by reliably doing what's expected of you and not raising any false expectations.

Trustworthiness is part and parcel of integrity, but in a management context it deserves special attention. If you are a manager you are, by definition, part of a collective enterprise, and a collective enterprise can only function at all if there is some level of trust between its members. In some cases, as in the armed forces, there is really no option other than to trust people completely. Soldiers in battle have to trust to the orders of their commanders, and the commanders have to trust to their orders being carried out. Lives depend on it. In most management situations the demands are less severe, but no organization can survive, let alone prosper, if nobody trusts anybody else.

At one level, this is not usually a problem. Few people are deliberately untrustworthy, and in all sorts of everyday matters we can routinely expect both to trust and to be trusted. Every time we venture out on the roads, for example, we trust in the behaviour of other road users and are trusted by them in turn. While that mutual trust is deeply rooted in human nature, however, it is also a matter of statistics, and forced on us by anonymity. Knowing nothing about the other drivers as individuals, we rely on the fact that most drivers, most of the time, can indeed be trusted.

In a management situation, people get to know whom they are dealing with and make their judgements accordingly. If you are a manager, people will generally assume that you have a basic level of trustworthiness, corresponding to what they expect from any sane and more or less reasonable person. But they will not necessarily assume that you can be trusted on specific tasks or issues that call for particular levels of skill, judgement or integrity. In the same way we might trust someone to drive a car but not to race it competitively (requiring a particular skill); to be generally decent and well-intentioned but not to be completely unprejudiced; to communicate a message but not to communicate it with complete accuracy, or with sensitivity.

So you have to win people's trust. You have to convince the people who work for you to trust your judgement on how to respond to the challenges faced by the unit. You have to convince them to trust you to speak for them in the wider organization. And you have to convince them to trust you to treat them all fairly in the case of disputes, mistakes or tightening budgets. In the same way, you have to convince the people you work for (senior managers, owners, directors or trustees) to trust you to make sound and considered decisions or recommendations; to act in the interests of the organization as a whole, and not just in those of your unit or yourself; and to get on with your job responsibly without too much interference.

The key to all this is solid and consistent reliability, especially at the personal level. No manager can get everything right when it comes to strategy or business judgements, but you can do your conscientious best, and you can be reliably decent, honest and openly fair. All these will earn you trust.

5 TRUST OTHER PEOPLE AS MUCH AS YOU CAN

The flip side of being trustworthy – trusting other people – is more tricky. We all know that some people just cannot be trusted, and it would seem negligent to assume that they can be. Indeed, much of business economics, and the tools and techniques based on it, start out from the assumption that people will act in their own self-interest, even if this involves cheating and deception, and that you would do better to trust in this rule of behaviour than to trust in people themselves. The received business school wisdom is, in effect, that you should trust in people's untrustworthiness.

We get a different perspective, however, from mathematical game theory, which explores patterns of cooperation in competitive situations. This suggests that your best strategy is generally to start out by trusting the other person and to distrust them if, and only if, your trust is not rewarded. This strategy delivers better results than either distrusting them from the beginning or trusting them regardless.

This makes intuitive sense. In all areas of life, the best results are achieved when people can, and do, trust each other, so you need to give it a go. But it would be folly to systematically put your trust in someone you know, on the basis of hard evidence, to be untrustworthy.

Game theory models describe very artificial situations in which the conditions remain unchanged from one period, or one decision, to the next. Life is rarely like that, however, and, as a manager, you will face many different situations. The basic rule still holds. You should start out by trusting people and continue doing so unless you have good reason to think them untrustworthy. But the critical question will not be simply, 'Is Bill trustworthy?' it will be, 'Can I trust Bill in this particular situation?'.

With some people, you find you can trust them at some times but not at others: when they have been drinking, for example, or get swamped by personal or family problems. With others it's a question of how much things matter to them. If you ask them to do something that they think is important, you can generally trust them to do it responsibly, but if it's something they don't think matters, they will be lazy, cut corners or not give it their full attention. Some people can be trusted to do things if they serve their own self-interest, but not if they don't. Others can be trusted only when they feel that other people depend on them. And, of course, everybody has their particular strengths and weaknesses and can be trusted more in situations that play to their strengths and less in those that play to their weaknesses.

Everybody is different and, as a manager, you will gradually

Example 6: Trust

Trust and respect are closely linked. Trust breeds respect and vice versa, and what builds or damages one, generally builds or damages the other. Competent in their jobs, loyal to their staff and inherently trustworthy, both George, the garage branch manager, and Melanie, the hospital matron, are trusted as well as respected by both staff and superiors.

Ed, the managing director, has had to work harder to gain people's trust, especially where the trade unions were concerned. He has often had to implement policies devised at headquarters and was easily branded as 'them' ('management') rather than 'us' ('workers'). He has also had, on occasion, to stand up for his workforce in the face of short-sighted or uninformed corporate policies, and this has put a strain on his relationship with his superiors. Like many managers, he is sometimes caught in the middle, needing the trust of both staff and superiors to mediate effectively, but at risk of losing both. The best way to deal with this, he has found, is by being scrupulously honest and straightforward. People don't always like him as a result, but they do tend to trust him, and at the end of the day, that matters more.

learn whom you can trust, when and under what circumstances. The golden rule, however, is to always start out by presuming that you can trust them, because that's the only way you'll find out whether you can or not. If you trust someone and they don't deliver, you've at least learnt something useful. If you start out by not trusting someone who could, in fact, have been trusted, you'll have no way of knowing that and will lose a potentially valuable resource.

The other question that arises in this connection is whether and how you might engender trustworthiness in people. There are clearly ways of getting people to do things reliably that don't involve trustworthiness as such. As with getting people to listen, you can get them to act as you want if they are frightened of the consequences of doing otherwise, or else desperate to please. But these approaches damage rather than enhance their capabilities and a good manager will resort to them only as a last resort. To build people's trustworthiness you have to get them to see the value

In Polly's case, and also in Rick's, building trust and building respect have gone hand in hand. A headmistress cannot do her job unless she is trusted, not only by staff and governors but by parents as well, and in Polly's exposed position, integrity is everything. She can never please everybody with every decision, but she is building a reputation for being fair and reasonable, for always fulfilling her promises and for putting the children's interests first. Rick's responsibilities are less daunting and he is much less exposed to the world outside his small organization, but the general principles are the same.

When it comes to trusting other people, George has no problem and Ed, Polly and Melanie, for different reasons, have no choice. If a teacher, nurse or other professional can't be trusted, then they shouldn't be a teacher or nurse. Both Polly and Melanie have to carefully monitor and tutor their charges (and also the ancillaries, cleaners and so on, who make their environments safe and healthy) but they can't always be on top of them and have to start out from a position of trust. In Ed's case the business is just too big for him to be on top of it all, so he has to trust others to manage for him and to judge them largely by their results – by performance measures on the one hand and the absence of grievances on the other.

of trusting relationships, and you can do this best by being trust-worthy yourself and by demonstrating your trust in them, however limited this may be. When they realize that they are being trusted, and that however unimportant they might consider the task, fulfill-ing that trust matters to you, most people will respond positively. If you're prepared to trust people in small matters, you'll often find that they become trustworthy in larger ones. Trust feeds on trust, and is wrecked by distrust.

6 NOBODY'S PERFECT – NOT EVEN YOU

Human beings are remarkable creatures. From logic to loving, we have all sorts of wonderful and amazing capabilities. But we are also 'only human'. We succumb to temptation. We lose attention. We cut corners. We take the easy option. We make mistakes and misjudgements. As a manager, you always need to keep in mind the often surprising extent of people's potential, and respect and trust are important parts of this. But you also need to keep in mind their fallibility. No human being is perfectly competent. Nobody gets it right all the time.

This is important both when setting people tasks and targets, and when assessing how well they have performed. As a general rule, you will want to set people targets that stretch them. This is how you build up their capabilities, to everyone's advantage, and it is how you improve the performance of your unit. When the opportu-nity arises, you will also want to set them some tasks that they find challenging. This gives them an opportunity to learn and develop, and it keeps them interested and engaged in their work. A new chal-lenge is stimulating in itself; and the chance to demonstrate learning and achievement focuses people on the possibilities of recognition and promotion if they perform well.

There is no point, however, in basing the tasks and targets you set on unreal or unreasonable expectations. You need to leave some room for accident or error. If you ask people to do some-thing they are just not competent to do, you will only disaffect them and damage what competence and confidence they have. If you put them in a position where a small misjudgement, of the kind people make all the time, wrecks everything, you risk breaking them, not stretching them.

When it comes to assessing people's performance, you need to be careful not to reprimand or punish them for not doing what you couldn't reasonably have expected them to do. You need to make allowance not only for circumstances and events, but also for human nature. People who are charged with making repeated life and death decisions – air traffic controllers might be an example – work limited hours and receive intensive training and psychological support. Most workers are not supported in that way and when they have had a bad night or have something on their mind, they quite naturally and quite routinely perform below the level they might achieve under 'perfect' conditions. To expect otherwise is unreasonable, unfair and quite unproductive.

It is also important that you don't mistake a simple lack of competence for something more sinister: intentional shirking or wilful non-performance, for example. If a task seems quite easy and straightforward to you, it can be hard to understand why somebody else should find it so difficult, and quite easy to jump to the conclusion that they are being negligent or obstructive. This is not usually the case, however, and if it is, there will be reasons for it. Indeed, obstructiveness is often a mask for incompetence, as people struggle to admit, even to themselves, that a task is beyond them. When people underperform it is usually because they aren't up to the job, not because they choose to underperform. In much the same way, when a team project goes astray, it is much more likely to be due to a cock-up than to a conspiracy.

The other thing that's really important to remember here is that when the people who work for you do underperform, it may be as much – or more – your fault as theirs. You are human too. You make your own misjudgements and mistakes, as we all do, and sometimes the problems that people get into when working for you are a consequence of those.

It may be, for example, that your instructions were incorrect or, more likely, just confused. It is so, so easily done! You may, without realizing it, have given mixed messages that people struggled to reconcile and interpret. You may have asked too much of people. You may have asked too little. Or you may have asked it in the wrong way, unintentionally upsetting people by your manner or by the language you used, or otherwise compromising their ability to do a good job.

The famous psychologist, C. J. Jung, once observed that if you see a psychological problem in a child, you should look first to the parents, who have probably brought it about, loading the child with their own anxieties and neuroses. If, as a manager, you see a problem with the performance of someone who works for you, you should look first to yourself and ask: 'Have I partly brought this on by what I have said and done?'.

7 ADMIT TO YOUR MISTAKES – AND LEARN FROM THEM

Since you are only human and not perfect, you will make mistakes. If you've been to a business school, you may be forgiven for finding that a bit surprising. In the business school world, mistakes simply don't exist. Management theories take no account of them and, while an analysis can be faulty, the remedy there is just to do a better analysis. No attention is paid to the situation where you have made a faulty analysis and are now stuck with the consequences, let alone to the kinds of non-analytical mistakes we all make all of the time.

Many managers never do make mistakes – in their own minds! When anything goes wrong, it is always due to bad luck, circumstances beyond their control or somebody else's fault. It is never their fault. This is understandable. None of us like admitting we've got it wrong, even to ourselves, and we are all biased in favour of our own judgement over other people's. Some people, maddeningly, almost always are right. But nobody gets things right all of the time and all of us, if we're really honest with ourselves, make far more mistakes than we would like to admit.

As this last observation suggests, there are two issues here: recognizing our mistakes, or acknowledging them to ourselves, and admitting them to other people. Let us take them in that order.

Recognizing your own mistakes is not easy, but it is immensely valuable. It's not easy because it requires you to think carefully and hard in a detached, reflective way. This is something we mostly shy away from, because we know subconsciously that the things we are likely to discover will make us uncomfortable. And it is something that, as a manager, you will have precious little time for. If you are emotionally resistant to doing something, and you have a good reason for not doing it, then it becomes extremely difficult to do. It's immensely valuable, however, precisely because it requires you to think carefully and hard in a detached, reflective way! That is how you learn about yourself and your capabilities. It is how you overcome your limitations and become, among other things, a better manager. It won't prevent you from making mistakes, but it will help you not to make the same mistakes. It will improve your powers of judgement and, in understanding yourself and your mistakes much better, you will also get a much better understanding of other people and their mistakes.

The question as to whether and when you should admit your mistakes to other people is a difficult one. The principles of honesty and integrity point to owning up, but there are clearly many cases in which this would be counterproductive. If your mistake has passed unnoticed, for example, and no-one has suffered as a result, then telling people about it might damage your credibility and your managerial performance, without achieving any gain. One of the ways we get through life, and work, with reasonable efficiency is by accepting certain tolerance levels. We don't expect people's use of words, for example, to be perfectly precise, but just to do the job of communication that is required. Similarly with actions and judgements, if we were too pernickety, nothing would ever get done. So while you should always seek to learn from your own mistakes, it's not always appropriate to burden others with the telling of them.

At the other end of the scale, however, there are cases where you clearly should own up. If, for example, your keeping quiet would mean somebody else getting blamed, that would be grossly unfair on the somebody else. It would also be damaging to the organization, which would proceed and 'learn' on the basis of a faulty diagnosis. Moreover, even if there is no risk of someone else getting blamed, the risks associated with a faulty diagnosis might make it imperative that you own up, for purely practical reasons, for the sake of the organization as a whole and for that of the unit you manage. And it may be too that other people could learn from your mistake, if they only knew about it.

Where you draw the line between situations in which it is better to own up and situations in which it is better to keep quiet – assuming always that you own up to yourself – is hard to say. Since all the psychological pressures push in the direction of keeping quiet, however – to protect your reputation, avoid being blamed, etc. – you should almost certainly allow for a bias in that direction. This means that, if you are in any doubt, you should own up, at least to your own manager or boss. Whether your admission should be more public than that is probably for them to decide.

8 FORGIVE OTHER PEOPLE'S MISTAKES AND DEAL WITH THEM CONSTRUCTIVELY

Just as you will inevitably make mistakes from time to time, so will other people. Sometimes mistakes will be made by your own bosses, or elsewhere in the organization, and all you can do will be to play your part in rescuing the situation. As a general rule it is for your bosses to tell you they've messed things up, not for you to tell them. It is a different matter, though, when mistakes are made by the people who work for you. Then you have a responsibility not only to put things right, but also to respond appropriately in your management of the people concerned.

Let us assume that a mistake has been made in your unit and that it was not primarily your mistake. You have reflected on the situation and satisfied yourself that you haven't given unclear instructions, or asked too much of someone, or been negligent in your supervision. Something has gone wrong and it's pretty clear that someone, let's call him Dave, has made a mistake. How should you respond?

The first rule, very simply, is to forgive him. Don't harbour a grudge. There are two reasons for this. One is because he is a human being and making mistakes is one of the things that make us human. We forgive all sorts of things in our friends, and we do so because, being close to them, we recognize their humanity and make allowances. In this sense friendship is a model relationship and you should treat anybody who works for you as if they were a friend – not with familiarity, but with sympathy and understanding.

The second reason is because it's only once you have adopted an attitude of forgiveness that you can move on to understanding someone, understanding what went wrong and why, and learning from it. We often ignore this. We think that we should work out what went wrong first and then decide whether to forgive. But things don't work like that. Just as with trust and respect, you will only make progress if you start out with the presumption of forgiveness.

To forgive is not to forget, let alone to ignore. It is not a way of dismissing the problem, but a first step towards understanding what happened and working out what to do about it. Some mistakes can be more or less ignored, and others call for actions of various, quite different, kinds.

At one end of the scale there are mistakes that really are best ignored and passed over without comment. There are those one-off little slips – and some not-so-little slips – that arise from peculiar circumstances that are unlikely to recur. Dave forgot to do something because his mother had just gone into hospital and his mind was a bit all over the place, as would be the case with any normal healthy human being. Don't even mention it. Also in this category are those cases where there is no need for your intervention. Dave has made a mistake but you can see that he has recognized that himself, he is addressing the cause and is trying to learn from it. You may need at some future time to commend him for his improvement, but you are probably better not to say anything now. Let him get on with it.

Moving up the scale, suppose now that Dave has not only forgotten to do something once or twice but is beginning to make a habit of it: he is generally preoccupied with his mother's health and his work is suffering as a result. Or suppose that he has made a mistake that he could learn from, but that he isn't recognizing the fact or isn't learning. In these cases you should say something. You should bring the matter to his attention, quietly and in a supportive way, and perhaps help him to address it. You might give him some advice, if you have the relevant experience, and some support. You might undertake to keep an eye on him – to monitor him, but in a constructive mentoring way, not a disciplinary one.

So far we have focused on informal responses, but sometimes something more formal is needed. It may be, for example, that Dave could benefit from some formal training. Perhaps his mistakes are due to gaps in his technical competence, or he hasn't fully grasped issues of data protection or health and safety, or he lacks confidence and would benefit from some training in interpersonal skills.

Continuing further up the scale, it may be that things are more serious and that Dave not only lacks competence in a key area, but is unlikely to ever achieve the level of competence needed, if the work of the unit as a whole and the careers of his colleagues are not to suffer. In a large organization this will involve competency proceedings and a detailed paper trail of documented mistakes, warnings and training courses. He will have to be given every possible opportunity to acquire the competence he lacks. In a smaller organization it may just be a question of parting company with a generous payoff or of demotion to a less demanding job, but even here you have to be very careful about the procedures you go through.

Much the same applies in cases of disciplinary action. It might be that Dave is making mistakes because he is deliberately obstructive or skiving off, wilfully negligent or not following instructions. In a small, private sector organization, your best bet may well be to just part company, whatever it costs, but in a large corporation or agency you will have to follow a route of escalating procedures, beginning with informal warnings and moving through written warnings to formal hearings. What is important here is that you act straight away. There is always a temptation to hope that the problem will go away or that it will cease to be your problem, so you don't take any formal actions. Then when things get worse, or when another manager takes over, there is nothing on the record and everything has to be started from scratch. Dave continues to cause problems for everyone, and because the issue is never escalated, he never gets the counselling or other help he almost certainly needs.

Example 7: Mistakes

All of the managers we have met so far have to deal with mistakes, both their own and others, and in some cases this is an important part of their job. In a hospital context, for example, even quite small mistakes can have serious consequences for patient health, but in an environment where many staff are over-worked and under pressure, mistakes are inevitable. One of Melanie's responsibilities as a matron is to ensure that any mistakes made on the wards are kept to a minimum and that they are corrected before any serious damage is done.

To explore the question of mistakes a bit more, let's meet another manager, Brad. Brad runs his own small building firm, B. B. Builders, working on domestic new buildings, extensions, conversions and renovations. He started the firm eight years ago and now employs about a dozen people in all.

In the building trade, as everyone knows, mistakes happen. Indeed they happen all the time. Some are easily put right. Some get covered up (not always intentionally!) and only become manifest years later. Some cause major headaches, landing clients with unwelcome and sometimes costly delays and landing someone – often both the builder and the client – with the costs of putting them right.

To deal with mistakes, Brad has adopted a set of simple rules:

1. Keep a very close eye on things. Before he set up on his own he had worked for a larger firm where the boss had decided

So some mistakes need to be passed over without comment. Others need to be clamped down on hard. But all should be forgiven and all should be dealt with both carefully and constructively.

9 KNOW YOUR COSTS AND LEARN HOW TO CONTROL THEM, BUT DON'T BECOME OBSESSED WITH THEM

So far in this part of the book we have focused on managing people and managing through people. It's time now to turn to information, and the most important information in any business, and in almost any managed organization, is basic accounting information. If the first rule of managing people is 'know yourself', the aphorism

to save money by dispensing with a project manager. The resulting mistakes had cost him far more than he saved, never mind the loss of goodwill from unhappy clients. Brad's firm was still too small for a full-time project manager but he and his number two between them checked on every site every day.

2. When a mistake is discovered, put it right immediately. If it's at all serious, tell the client and apologize. Sometimes mistakes arise because a builder misunderstands a client's request, and sometimes that's as much or more the client's fault as the builder's. Financial negotiations are inevitable. But always admit some role in the error. Never blame the client entirely or, for that matter, the employee concerned.

3. Internally, treat all mistakes as teaching and learning opportunities. If employees don't learn, they will have to go, but don't expect professional standards of carefulness from staff who have never been taught them.

4. If the mistake is even partly yours (and although he was reluctant to admit it, Brad did still make mistakes himself, misreading a specification, garbling or rushing through an instruction, glossing over poor work or losing his temper on site), take all the blame on yourself.

The question is, how good a set of rules are these? Brad is sure that his approach is better than trying to deny mistakes and blame them on others, but he isn't at all sure that it is the best approach. What do you think?

inscribed at the entrance to the ancient Temple of Apollo at Delphi, the first rule of managing information is 'know your costs'.

Our attitudes to costs are strange. We sometimes get obsessed by them but often ignore them completely. The two are connected. When costs are ignored, they tend to rise and to keep on rising until the viability of the organization is put under threat. Panic then sets in and there's a massive drive to cut costs, or rather to cut other people's costs – often those initiating the drive have a strange tendency to exempt themselves from its consequences!

Business schools have also done their bit to make things worse. Courses in production management tend to excite people with the dramatic cost-cutting possibilities of business process re-engineering. Courses in marketing proceed as if costs simply didn't exist. Courses in strategy or general management, which used to take a company's detailed accounts as the starting point for a comprehensive analysis, nowadays leave them out, probably because the teachers can't understand them themselves. So students never get to take a balanced view and never learn the basic discipline of cost control.

Whatever kind of organization you work in, the unit you manage will in effect be a cost centre. It will have a budgeted total expenditure, divided into a number of categories. This won't necessarily be written down. Your unit may be amalgamated for accounting purposes with others or the organization may not have a formal system of management accounting. And you won't necessarily be able to control all, or even any, of the costs. You may, for example, have the authority to hire temporary staff but not to hire or fire permanent employees; to take people on but not to decide their pay rates; to purchase small items but not large ones. There may well be general overhead costs, for buildings and maintenance, say, that are simply imposed on the unit. But even if you aren't given the discretion to make expenditure decisions yourself, you will be the person with access to the information needed if those decisions are to be well made.

Everything your unit does comes with a cost: the salaries and wages of people, the spaces they occupy, the materials and equipment they use, the goods they process and the spaces those occupy, heat and light, repairs and maintenance, travel and training, and so on. To manage effectively you need a clear handle on what those costs are and why, how they are changing and why. If you're given a formal budget, you need to make sure you understand it. What exactly does this item refer to? Why has that one gone up 10 per cent since last year? Why am I being charged for this but not for that? If you don't have a written budget, it is a very good idea to create one. You may not be able to get exact figures, but even an approximate breakdown of your unit's expenditure will help you enormously to understand how it works, and where its problems might lie.

Once you know your costs, you can begin to control them in an intelligent way, whether directly or through recommendations and requests to your own bosses. Why, you might ask, are we spending on this when we didn't seem to need it before? Do we still need to be doing that, or buying that? Should we be rebalancing our spending as the relative costs of different services or supplies change?

Good managers know and understand their costs, and they keep them under control, but they don't get obsessed by them. The old adage 'look after the pennies and the pounds will look after themselves' makes perfect sense if you are struggling in poverty, but much better advice for managers is to heed the warning 'penny wise, pound foolish'. Cutting down on the office biscuits won't make any difference to your cost base. It might well serve to convey an important message – times are tight – but you can do that much more effectively by moderating your own personal expenditure. And it will almost certainly make people grumpy and unproductive, costing far more than it saves. The same thing often happens with small so-called efficiency improvements. The costs you save are easily measurable but very small. The costs you incur are much harder to measure accurately (lower motivation, poorer communications, lowered customer satisfaction), but much, much greater. Staff cuts too can often be unproductive, as you save on wages but lose on knowledge and commitment, and end up paying a fortune on agency fees.

You don't generally need to measure costs really accurately, and the more comfortable and familiar you get with your budgets, the less you will worry about the precise numbers. What you do need is to have a rough and ready picture of all your costs and how they interrelate.

10 UNDERSTAND HOW YOUR UNIT ADDS VALUE AND EXPLORE HOW IT COULD ADD MORE

The other side of costs is revenues, but these are often much harder to estimate. In a complex organization it is usually possible to allocate costs between different departments – not perfectly, as facilities and resources will often be shared and some overheads may have to be estimated, but more or less effectively. It can be much harder to allocate revenues, because what people are paying for is not the parts but the whole. In some contexts, if you are managing a shop or a restaurant, for example, many of your costs will be fixed and the revenues will be critical. But if you are managing an administrative office, or a civil service department, or one small part of a larger operation, you might well have no idea what revenues your unit earns. The best way to look at this side of the equation is, therefore, through another, more flexible, concept: added value.

Whatever the unit you manage does, it must be adding value or generating something of value, for some end-user. If it isn't, there is no economic justification for its existence – or for yours as its manager. To manage the unit effectively you need to know what that value is, how it is being generated, and the part played by each

Example 8: Costs and Benefits

Of the managers we have considered so far, some evidently have more control over their costs than others. Brad, running his own building firm, has almost total control over what he spends. Rick is more constrained, as many of his fixed costs (rent, rates, decor, etc.) are dictated by the choices of the restaurant owner, but he still has very wide discretion and, like Brad, he needs to use it carefully. Both have to know their costs in intimate detail, and couldn't be in control of their business otherwise. At the other end of the spectrum, Polly and Melanie are much more constrained. Both have to work within budgets set by other people, and those budgets are dominated by costs and revenues incurred by other people: above all by staff salaries and overheads and income streams that are effectively fixed. Ed and George are somewhere in the middle. Their organizations set tight constraints in terms of expected profit margins, but they can nevertheless influence both income and expenditure.

There is a similar spectrum in terms of value added. For both Melanie and Polly, the value their teams add, in successful births and children's education, is very hard to measure financially. For George and Ed, selling relatively standardized products, value added is much more straightforward. In this case Brad and Rick are in the middle, as what bring in their revenues are not just house extensions or meals but the customer experiences that go with those.

We shall be using the examples of a school, a restaurant, a maternity unit and a garage branch to illustrate some of the techniques that can be used to assess costs and value added in the third part of the book, so to illustrate the basic concepts let's consider Brad's building firm.

Running his own business, Brad potentially has full control over his costs, but this has not been easy to achieve in practice. When he had started out it had been with the conviction that he could easily beat the competition on both cost and quality, but he had seriously underestimated the overhead costs involved in a business: rent and rates, equipment and services, and above all down-time due to cancelled projects, bad weather and all sorts of other causes. Now, eight years in, he knows his costs inside out and has worked out how to keep them under control. He has also learnt a lot, some of it the hard way, about value added: what people most value in a building project and what they are prepared to pay for. And he has begun to work out how this can be delivered, not only through his quality building, but also through little things like politeness, keeping clients informed, and hosing down and sweeping up at the end of every day. These touches have done wonders for the firm's reputation and hence for the prices he can charge.

For a manager working in a large organization, things are very different. Let's meet Belle, who is a branch manager at British Bank – not nowadays the pillar of a town community as bank managers once were, but a relatively low-level manager in a very large, bureaucratic organization. Belle has very little control over her costs. Her branch is equipped and supplied and her staffing levels are set by central departments. The value added is also hard to gauge. She gets management accounts, which purport to show the branch's costs and revenues, but now that there is little correlation between the services provided at branch level and the profits earned from customers whose accounts are nominally located at that branch, the accounts convey very little.

In this context, Belle's main reference point is what the bank promotes, both in its internal communications and through its advertising, as the general basis of its added value, and this combines two contrasting elements. On one hand, there are the bank's systems, built around impersonal efficiency and designed above all to minimize costs. On the other hand, there is a strongly promoted image of personal customer service. In theory, these two elements should be complementary but, in practice, they are often in tension. Employees are trained to be friendly and helpful, and are friendly and helpful, but they are often unable to help, because the systems won't let them. And when they can help, by selling loans, mortgages, insurance products or premium-priced banking services – sometimes seen as their main function – they often lack the technical knowledge to understand what they are selling and so give advice that, from a professional point of view, they should not be giving. A significant part of Belle's role as a manager is to manage this tension at the branch level. Her staff can't always add value for the customer, but by leading and coaching them she can at least ensure that they don't take it away.

of your people and processes. This is not an exact science. Value is often generated by people and processes working together, across different parts of the organization. It may well be that what Jill does in your unit is unseen by the customer but helps Jack, in another unit, do something that is seen. You often can't quantify the benefits from such interconnections, and there may be little point in trying, but you do need to be aware of them.

The first question you will ask in this context is whether such and such a process or activity is adding any value at all. It sometimes happens that organizations keep doing things they always have done, or in the way they always have done them, even when these no longer add any useful value. It also happens that they try doing new things in the hope of adding value, that these never really achieve anything, but that they keep on going regardless. On the other hand, the ways in which an organization does add value often get taken for granted or lost from sight. So, if some activity looks, on the face of it, to be redundant, you should always look much more carefully at how it connects with, and supports, other activities.

The next question is whether the value added is plausibly in line with the cost incurred. Once again this is not a question of detailed calculation. But if you know and understand your cost base, you should be able to look at what is being achieved in terms of value added and ask, 'Does this make sense? Or are we, perhaps, because of changes in our customers' needs or changes in our own cost base, spending a lot of money to generate little in the way of value?' If so, that is something you may need to analyse more carefully, or take to your own bosses.

Finally, you will want to explore how your unit could add more value. Could any of the unit's processes, skills and knowledge be put to better use? Could you serve your customers, or other units of the organization, more effectively, without adding to your costs, by doing things in a different way? It might just be a question of turning things round faster, or being more helpful or accessible. It might be a question of sharing information or making it more readily available. It might be a question of providing the service people need now rather than the one they needed last year.

None of this is straightforward. It all involves finding out about what people do value; and from where you sit in the organization that might be difficult. It shouldn't be difficult, though, if the organization as a whole is to flourish. The most effective organizations are those in which everyone understands the value-adding proposition and the part they can play in it. So pushing for the information will often be a valuable service in itself, providing it is done diplomatically. And within the unit itself, the aim of serving people better is always a motivating force.

11 UNDERSTAND HOW YOUR ORGANIZATION WORKS: WHAT IS VALUED, ASSUMED, EXPECTED?

Costs, revenues and value added are critical for any organization, and for any unit within an organization. But they are not the only things on which your unit – and by implication your own performance – will be judged. You also need to take account of values in the other sense of the word: the cultural values or social norms of the organization, what it assumes, what it expects and what it does or doesn't value in terms of the behaviour of its members.

It's been fashionable in recent years to appoint experienced businessmen or businesswomen to run civil service departments, government agencies, universities, arts companies and other notfor-profit organizations that traditionally appointed their senior managers from within. The thinking is that private sector businesses are generally more efficient, more disciplined, more entrepreneurial and better at serving customer needs – they have to be to flourish in a competitive environment – and that the new appointments will bring these skills and values with them.

It doesn't generally work. There are some successes, of course, but what generally happens is that the incomers leave after a few years, having achieved nothing except some unproductive antagonism, and frustrated that the organization has resisted and disrupted their attempts to manage 'properly'.

In such situations, there is usually a taking of sides and each side then blames the other for what has gone wrong. By and large, however, the people appointed are quite competent managers, at least in a business context, and the people they try and fail to manage are not intentionally disruptive. But if you are to manage an organization effectively, you have to understand what makes it tick. And that means more than just understanding the general theory: you have to know it inside out, to feel it in your bones. This takes time as well as effort and, if the culture is an alien one, it can be very hard. It is no wonder that business executives aren't very good at running universities: university professors, even if they were business school professors, wouldn't be much good at running businesses either. For the same reasons, people with a production background aren't generally very good at running marketing-based companies, and people from a marketing background aren't very good at running engineering companies.

You begin to understand how an organization works the day you join it. You begin by learning the little things, like attitudes to coffee breaks, what people do for lunch, how they address each other. You learn the organizational language: the acronyms, the slang. And you go on to learn the patterns of meetings and reports. You learn what is compulsory and what is taboo, and how the organization deals with routine processes like hiring and firing, training and discipline. You couldn't manage at all without a lot of this knowledge.

To be an effective manager, to manage well, you need to do more than just learn what you have to. You need to study the organization. Work out how all these things fit together. Look too at the physical spaces (architecture, furniture), the information systems, the brands and symbols. And try and work out from all this, the core values that drive the organization.

Sometimes these values may be in the process of changing. Sometimes you may need to challenge them. But you can only do this, or contribute to a change programme, if you fully understand how things work now: what matters, what is expected, what is assumed. Much of what goes on in any organization is a product of habit, of established practices and routines, and of taken-for-granted assumptions that people aren't consciously aware of. It's as if people were governed in their behaviour by some kind of mysterious computer program. As a manager wishing to have an effect on what people do and how they do it, you need to understand how that program operates.

12 THINK CAREFULLY ABOUT PERFORMANCE MEASURES: WHAT IS MEASURED IS WHAT YOU WILL GET

One of the things that ties together cost, value added and the cultural values of an organization is its system of performance measurement and performance management.

The simplest systems of performance management are piece rates, whereby workers get paid in direct proportion to their output, and flat wages or salaries, where people get paid by the hour or week, regardless of what they achieve. Piece rates are commonplace in simple manual work: so miners get paid according to how much coal they dig or agricultural workers according to how much fruit they pick. They are also commonplace in sales: sales representatives might just be paid commissions on what they sell. Or they might get a basic wage, topped up by commission. Factory workers on a production line might have their performance very closely monitored through 'time and motion' studies, with a basic wage dependent on performance targets being met and bonuses providing an incentive for beating those targets.

White collar workers outside sales, from clerical workers to managers and professionals, have traditionally been paid fixed wages or salaries, often with no attempt to measure their performance. Over the last few decades, however, performance targets of one kind or another have been introduced for most employees, including managers, in most kinds of organization. If you manage a unit in a large or medium-sized organization, the performance of the unit will probably be measured in terms of some set of 'key performance indicators', or KPIs, and your own performance as a manager will be assessed either in terms of meeting benchmark targets for each indicator or in terms of your progress towards meeting those targets.

Performance measures can be of many different kinds. Typical measures include how much individuals or organizational units process or produce, how much they sell, how much profit they generate or how their performance is rated by customer surveys. These can be combined in different ways, however, and they can be broken down into finer measures: what proportion of tasks of a particular kind were completed within so many days, for example. And special kinds of organization are subject to special kinds of measurement. Hospital performance is measured in terms of waiting times, patient turnover and bed occupancy rates, for example; school performance in terms of test and exam results.

Performance measures can also be relative. So individual performances might be measured against those of a peer group, and the performance of an organization unit might be measured against the performance of other units in the organization, or similar units in comparable or competing organizations. Or the measures used might be adjusted to take account of circumstances. A salesman working in a prosperous region, for example, might be measured on different criteria from one working in a depressed region, where sales are much harder to achieve.

Performance measures are also used in different ways. Sometimes they act just as a management tool: if the targets are not met, people are called to account by their managers and remedial measures agreed upon. If they are met and exceeded, the door is opened to possible promotion. In other cases they are linked to incentive payments: either cash bonuses or shares in a company.

This measuring and managing of people's performance has obvious advantages, and over the last twenty years it has become something of an obsession. If you want to improve the performance of an organization, it makes sense to try and improve the performance of its members, and you can only work out how to improve it if you have some way of measuring what it is. If you then assume that people are basically self-interested and financially motivated, it makes sense to tie their measured performance in to their pay packets.

All this assumes, however, that performance can be relatively easily measured. In practice, for a great many jobs, performance is a very complex phenomenon and can't be reduced to simple quantitative measures. Many employees are engaged in multiple tasks, and while these might be listed in a job specification, there's almost always a residual category amounting to 'whatever else may be needed', calling for flexibility and common sense. Moreover, while each specified task might be individually measurable, the balance between them, dependent on external circumstances and events, might not be.

There are other problems too. Sometimes incentivizing people to perform on economic measures (profit, turnover, speed) can carry ethical risks. If a unit developing new products is measured and paid according to the speed with which it launches them on the market, speed being necessary to beat the competition, or is set a benchmark price it has to keep to, important safety issues may be overlooked. If a servicing and repair unit, or a surgery unit, is measured according to how many repairs or operations it carries out, it may end up advising people that they need repairs and operations when they don't.

The relationship between individual and team performance is another source of problems. Someone who is determined to meet individual targets may be reluctant to help out others, lacking congeniality or even being disruptive, thereby reducing everybody else's performance. Where targets are set for a team, you may get resentment from the most capable members as they have both to carry the weaker members and see their own rewards held back by those weaker members.

There are problems too with financial incentives, which easily damage essential non-financial incentives, like the intangible rewards people get from the satisfaction of a job well done, from the altruistic support of others, from commitment to an organization or from the collegiality of a group who enjoy working together. If these kinds of motivations are dominant in an organization, of course, the financial incentives won't be very effective, but research shows that financial incentives generally drive out others. So the financial incentives do generally work, but at the cost of making people cynical rather than committed, self-interested rather than altruistic and calculating rather than engaged.

A good way of thinking about the impact of performance measures is in terms of the acronym WYMIWYG: What You Measure Is What You Get. As a general rule, if you set people a target based on a particular measure, they will perform on that measure, but they will tend to neglect other measures that are also important. To take a simple but familiar example from business, if you measure the performance of a unit by how much revenue it generates, it will usually generate a lot of revenue. But it will often do so by cutting prices, so that profit goes down. If you measure it by how much profit it makes, it will typically generate more profit, but by focusing on the high-profit items, it may not turnover as much business as it would have done otherwise, which could cause problems elsewhere in the organization. Well-designed systems of performance measurement try to get a balance between the criteria that matter for the particular organization concerned at any particular time, but there is always a trade-off between what you ideally want and what you can practically specify in advance. What you ideally want, in an uncertain and ever-changing world, is for people to respond intelligently to situations as they develop. But because you can never know in advance what those situations might be, you can't easily generate measures of that performance. All you can do in practice is to specify a set of performance measures that you hope will work most of the time, for most people, to get them working in the right direction.

13 TO MAKE PERFORMANCE MEASURES WORK, YOU HAVE TO MAKE THEM WORK

So how do you respond to all this as a manager? A lot depends on the extent to which the performance measures for your unit are set for you, and the extent to which you can set them for yourself. If you are managing a unit in a larger organization, you will probably find that the key performance indicators and targets are set for you, but you may well be asked for some input to the process by which they are set, so that the targets are, technically at least, 'agreed'. Similarly, when it comes to the ways in which the performance of individual members of the unit are measured, there will probably be some organization-wide standards, but some flexibility for you to negotiate targets within these.

To the extent that you have some choice over the performance measures used, you need to ask four main questions.

1. What measures correspond most closely to the value added, from an organizational perspective, by your unit? For this, of course, you need a good understanding of how your unit adds value.
2. Which measures have the power to motivate people, both individually and as a team, in ways that are productive for the unit and the organization? What you are looking for here are the measures that engage and excite people, that bond them together, and that are meaningful in the context of the organization's culture, values and ways of doing things. For this, you need a good understanding of how the organization works.
3. What measures might be unintentionally counter-productive? Think through the consequences of choosing any particular measure or combination of measures, to understand what could go wrong and what you will have to monitor to ensure it doesn't go wrong.
4. What target levels will be best for stretching people to perform? Set the targets too low and you will encourage complacency and under-performance. Set them too high and you will risk aggravation and demotivation.

To the extent that you have no choice in the performance measures used, you have to apply them, of course, but you also have to make them work. For this you need to make the same kind of analysis as you would if you could choose them yourself. In particular, you need to be aware of what they can achieve in a positive way, and of what they risk achieving in a negative way. You then need to manage people so as to maximize the positive and control or mitigate the negative effects.

An important part of this management process is framing the performance measures and targets within a compelling story about what the organization is trying to achieve through them. If you are devising the measures yourself, this will be part and parcel of how you devise them. If you are applying measures that have been imposed on you, and those measures have been well chosen, the story should more or less tell itself. But this won't always be the case. Because performance measurement tends to get a hold on people and become obsessive, it often follows its own logic and leaves behind the logic of what the organization is trying to achieve. In such cases your challenge, as a manager, is to reconnect it in some way, so as to make the system both meaningful and productive for the people having to work under it.

There is a tricky balance to be struck here between toeing the organizational line and making the measures work. You may think that the indicators or targets chosen are ill-conceived, but you cannot say that to the people who work for you, as they will only be demotivated as a consequence. You have to work with the measures and put on them as positive a gloss as you can. But you also have to show sensitivity and judgement in their application, to keep people as far as possible on the track of serving the organization's real needs, while at the same time preventing them from suffering any adverse consequences from this. You can't have people failing to get a bonus, say, because you diverted them from their performance targets.

This can be a tremendous challenge but it is a challenge that is quite typical of those facing managers in general. A fascinating aspect of the history of management is that managers have always been conceived by the workers as representing the bosses – the owners of capital or the state – and thus as their natural enemies, while they have always been conceived by the bosses as representing their own interests as employees – the managerial class – and thus as their natural enemies too. In fact what managers have to do is the complete opposite of this. They have to represent and consistently speak up for the owners (or in a large organization, their senior managers) to the workers, and to represent and consistently speak up for the workers to the owners. So if there is a problem with the performance measures, or with the strategy or with anything else handed down to you that doesn't make sense for your unit, you have to take that problem up with your superiors, on behalf of the unit. But within the unit you have to be an agent for your superiors, and implement as best you can what they have decreed.

14 BE AVAILABLE – BE PRESENT

Performance measures are not the only things that seem, in theory, to be quite technical matters but, in practice, call heavily on the interpersonal skills of managers. Other than in the armed services – and often in those too – people are naturally suspicious of anything coming from another part of the organization and anything imposed on them from above. Performance measures are quite often seen as tools of oppression and control, strategies as delusions, and rules relating to health and safety or information security as bureaucratic

Example 9: Performance and Performance Measures

For a simple illustration of performance measures and performance management, let's focus on Brad and his building firm. As we noted in the last example, Brad has a good command of his costs, of the way his firm adds value and of some of the organization values that help him deliver that – values associated with care, quality and a high level of customer service. It's his own company, so he has a free hand as to how he runs it and, in particular, a free hand when it comes to performance measures.

Brad doesn't have a sophisticated system of performance measurement and he doesn't need one. He can see how his employees are performing and can give feedback on that on a daily basis, as well as in regular appraisals. He had never heard of performance appraisals in the building trade, though he guessed that the big construction firms must have them, but he had learnt the basics from his wife Betty, who worked for the local authority, and he now reviews each employee once or twice a year, focusing on their technical skills, their attitudes to work, and their behaviour with clients and colleagues. He pays people on regular wages, roughly in line with the local competition but geared to encourage long-term loyalty, and with a trade-off in favour of job security rather than short-term earnings. This, he finds, appeals to the kind of people who will fit in with the kind of firm he wants. He also pays bonuses on completion of projects and these are effectively a distribution of the money set aside for snagging (the process of fault correction that follows any building project) but not needed (because there weren't many faults). Again this rewards the behaviours he is trying to encourage.

At the other end of the spectrum is Belle, the branch manager

nuisances. Workers often assume that managers are out to get them, and junior managers often presume that senior managers are out of touch and don't know what they're doing.

Whatever level of management you are in yourself, you have to overcome these barriers, and this brings us back to your personal and interpersonal skills. We have already discussed the importance of a mutuality of trust and respect, but what are some of the specific things you can do to help bring that about? And what can you do

at British Bank. We saw in the last example that there is a conflict between the way the bank tries to manage costs, through efficient impersonal systems, and the way it seeks to add value, through an image of personal customer service. This kind of tension might be resolved by strong organizational values but, in this case, it is just complicated by a further tension, between the values of a very traditional bank culture based around reliability, security and service, and those of the bank's investment banking arm, with a culture of aggressive risk-taking in pursuit of sales and performance.

This confusion is reflected in the bank's performance measurement systems and the way they are used. The key performance indicators emphasize sales, because the sales and the profits they generate can be measured. The general level of customer satisfaction is measured through telephone and online surveys, but whether the sales meet customers' needs doesn't get taken into account, because that is hard to measure. In keeping with the emphasis on sales, individual pay includes an element of incentives, over which Belle has little control.

Progress through the organization, however, is based largely on staff appraisals, and while these employ forms and procedures dictated by corporate HR, they do allow Belle to take some account, informally, of a wider range of factors. They also give her a mechanism for helping her staff to reconcile the competing values and competing pressures on them. Her aim is a branch in which staff generate profits by giving excellent and fully informed customer service, and not just by smiling and selling. By asking them to talk through the deals they have done or the services they have provided, she finds that she can guide them through explicit but essentially informal objectives, specific to each, as well as through more formal indicators.

to make sure that both you and the people who work for you have the information needed to understand the situation facing you (as opposed to relying on unfounded biases and assumptions) and to respond to it productively?

The first rule is simply to be there: be available – be present. Above all, be available to the people who work for you. Don't separate yourself off from them any more than you have to. The degree of separation appropriate will depend on the organization and its culture. An army officer will be expected to preserve a social distance from his troops, and in any organization getting too close to some people will run the risk of disaffecting others and of accusations of favouritism. But, if you are to manage a unit effectively, you need to know the people who work for you. You need to know their personalities, their relationships with each other, their particular strengths and areas for improvement, their hopes and fears, their foibles. You need to know what drives them: their motivations and ambitions. You also need to understand the work they do and, of course, how well they do it. Only with this knowledge can you set about improving the productivity of the team, mentoring the individuals in it and diagnosing what goes wrong when things do go wrong.

Looking at it from the point of view of the people who work for you, they also need to know something about you: about your ambitions and expectations, your values and attitudes, your tolerance levels and your sticking points. Above all they need to know that they can come to you with their problems and receive a hearing that is both sympathetic and informed. As a general rule, this is made much easier by a personal relationship, however slight. If they have chatted with you about their holidays or their family, and about your holidays and your family, they will feel much less intimidated about coming to you and sharing their concerns. If they have chatted with you informally about their work, they will be that much more comfortable discussing it more formally.

In making yourself available to your unit, and being amongst them, at least as far as is appropriate within the culture of the organization (or even perhaps a bit further – as far as is 'not inappropriate'), you are not only sharing valuable information and smoothing working relationships, you are also conveying a simple but important message: that they matter.

All this is easier said than done. Many managers implement an 'open door' policy only for people to complain that while the door is always open, the manager is never there. Many managers resolve to walk regularly around their units, getting to know people and chatting about their work, only to find that by the time they've dealt with whatever needs dealing with first, everybody has gone home.

The best way to deal with the first problem is to make sure that if you're not available when they want you, people can always see you, face to face, by informal appointment, within a relatively short space of time – a day, say, or, at most, a couple of days. There is a trade-off here between the positive message and informational advantages of immediate access on one hand, and the efficiency of a delayed reaction on the other. Many problems of the moment disappear after a few hours reflection, and while you will want to know of their existence, you may not want to know everything that you would get from an instant report.

The best way to deal with the second problem is to schedule time – and fairly generous time – for the walk around. Ideally, this should not be at the same time each week, because you need to come across people at different tasks and in different states of mind. If you only see some people first thing in the morning or others in the late afternoon, you might get a very misleading impression. It also helps if it appears spontaneous. These are not spot checks – on the contrary, the aim is an interaction in which both you and they are relaxed and at ease. But if people know you are coming in advance, they will not be relaxed. They will waste valuable time preparing for the visit and put up barriers that will hinder effective communication. So a good slug of time at more or less regular but random intervals, and as much informality as possible.

The rules that apply to your interactions with the people who work for you also apply to your interactions with colleagues and superiors. They need the same kind of information about you as you need about the people in your unit. You, in turn, need to understand their needs and expectations. You need to know what's going on elsewhere in the organization, and you will get this information much more quickly and efficiently if you can get it through informal networks, based on regular, informal contacts, than if you get it only through formal reports. You also need feedback on your own performance, and again this will be much more useful if you get it on a regular basis through informal conversations than if you get it only through periodic formal reviews. You should use other people's knowledge and experience to help you steer a course, not wait for advice – and judgement – until you're on the rocks.

In managing upwards, as well as in managing downwards, the message you give is also important. If you don't make the most of opportunities to interact with the managers of other units, you will give them, and more senior managers, the impression that you don't think those other units matter. They may not matter, directly, so far as the tasks of your own unit are concerned, but they do matter to the organization as a whole. You need to demonstrate a commitment to your own unit, but you need even more to demonstrate a commitment to the organization as a whole.

15 BE INQUISITIVE, ENCOURAGE INQUISITIVENESS, SHARE INFORMATION

The more you communicate informally with people, the greater will be your chance of getting the information you need when you need it. But you have to ask. Odd as it may seem, people are much more likely to volunteer information about their personal lives than about their work. If you can build up a relationship on the basis of what they are happy to talk about, you can encourage them to talk about other things; but they may still be nervous of revealing their weaknesses. And even when it comes to completely neutral information, we take so much for granted that it doesn't occur to us that other people might not know things, and might need to know them. So you have to ask.

There will be some things that you don't know, and that you know you need or want to know. When you first join an organization, many of these will be relatively trivial: where can I get a sandwich, how do I claim expenses, or whom do I call when my computer goes down? They might be important to the work of your unit, but still quite straightforward: who handles purchasing queries when Sally is away, or what is the procedure for dealing with a customer complaint? They might be much more subtle: what is the argument behind the recent strategy announcement, or why does it take the procurement office six days to process a request?

The rule here is to ask the question straight away – don't be shy. And above all, don't worry about displaying your ignorance. Nobody likes to appear ignorant and if you feel 'I should know that' and hold back in the hope that you will somehow find out without asking, you will only be digging a hole for yourself, getting yourself into a position where you can't ask a question, even though you need to know the answer. It's a bit like asking for directions when you're lost, something that many men, especially, find very hard to do. Delaying can only possibly make matters worse, and while the cost here is clear – you will be late for an appointment, say – the cost in the work context is much less so. You don't know what might result from a lack of information or how much trouble you might be getting yourself into.

There will be other information that you need, or at least would benefit from, but don't know that you need. There might be someone somewhere in the organization with knowledge that would be useful to you. Or there might be stories of the past or collective memories that would shed light on how things are done now, and how they might be done differently. To access this kind of information, you have to be inquisitive. Good managers always have their eyes and ears open, and they are always prompting people to tell them things. You may not be able to do anything immediately with the information you gain, but you would be surprised what comes in useful. It might be that a problem five years ago has left the senior management resistant to particular kinds of innovation, or that a unit whose work impacts on yours is in the middle of a re-organization. It might just be that Alan in accounts has an uncle working for one of your suppliers. So find out as much as you can, as soon as you can, about the unit, the organization and the context in which they operate.

The same advice applies equally to others, so you should also encourage inquisitiveness in the people who work for you. Encourage them to ask questions of each other; of people elsewhere in the organization whom they might meet socially, professionally or on training courses; and especially of you.

Some people are inquisitive but shy, or reserved. They don't ask questions, but not because they're uninterested. Help them to overcome their shyness. Volunteer information and prod them to respond by asking for more. If they get themselves into a situation where they haven't asked a question out of shyness, and have found it harder and harder to ask as their lack of knowledge has become an embarrassment, help them out. And when the question does come, don't respond by saying, 'Why didn't you ask earlier?' but by saying, 'I'm so glad you asked'.

Some people have few inhibitions but are simply uninterested in anything that doesn't relate directly to their immediate interests. They'll tell you all about themselves but never ask anything about you. They can talk but they can't listen. These people present a much harder challenge. You can take a horse to water but you can't make it drink; and you can take a man to information but you can't make him listen – not without a lot of personal skills' development anyway. But you may be able to alleviate the problem a little bit by mentoring. You can make yourself aware of the situation and prepare yourself for some of the consequences. And you can try to ensure that the person concerned is not isolated in his (and it probably will be 'his') bubble, but that there are people around who are more inquisitive and better listeners.

We noted earlier that sharing information, both up and down and side to side, is a key aspect of managing. Being proactive about it, inquiring and encouraging inquisitiveness, is a key aspect of managing well.

Example 10: Being In Touch

Think about any of the managers we have met, and the importance of being there and being inquisitive is fairly obvious. Polly, for example, the primary school head, needs to know what is going on in her classrooms, and to be hyper-alert for any problems affecting the children: learning difficulties, behavioural difficulties, bullying and so on. Brad the builder needs to be on site asking questions, keeping on top of what his men are doing and of any problems they may be facing, and making sure that the clients' needs, which inevitably change as the building takes shape, are being met. George is the glue that holds his garage dealership branch together and ensures that everyone works to the same ends. He just couldn't do that if he shut himself in his office all day. While the guiding principles are the same across the board, however, each manager's situation is different, so let's look at two of them more closely: Ed, the engineering subsidiary managing director, and Melanie, the hospital matron.

As a central point of contact between clinicians, technicians, nurses, administrators and service managers, Melanie would ideally like to be everywhere at once. That's not possible, of course, but fortunately in a hospital people move around a lot, and the people she most needs to liaise with often pass by her door. She has to move around a bit herself, to case meetings or management meetings, but she tries to be around as much as possible when doctors do their rounds and nurses come off shift. She uses these opportunities to ask questions – indeed people joke about the grilling they receive – and the knowledge and insights she gains also enable her to answer questions, or at least to point people to others who might answer them.

16 ALWAYS KEEP AN OPEN MIND

Inquisitiveness can help you and your team acquire and share information, but you need to remember that information is not the same as knowledge. For information to be of use, you first have to interpret it – to fit it into a story and make sense of it. This always involves various kinds of assumptions or hypotheses, and when interpreting things in everyday life (as opposed, say, to scientific research), these are largely unconscious. This means that the conclusions you draw from the information you gather can very easily be false or mislead-

As well as being inquisitive herself, Melanie also encourages her nurses to be the same. This is partly to develop their technical nursing skills, and their ability to recognize and respond to patient symptoms. But it's partly to foster a more general kind of caring. Nurses on the wards see and hear things, if they take the trouble to notice them, that doctors on brief visits can't. Sometimes these are narrowly medical, but sometimes they point to other issues, like the need for emotional support or family issues, that can't be treated in hospital but need to be addressed later by health visitors or social services.

Ed cannot possibly be as available and in the thick of things in the way that Melanie is. Like many senior managers his open door usually reveals an empty office, and when he's in the office he's usually in a meeting. He does try to 'manage by walking around', taking a tour of the factory floor or popping his head into product development or sales, but having set out to do this at least once a week, he finds that once a month is more typical, for all his efforts. He also tries to spend as much time as he can in headquarters and even in some of the other subsidiaries, but again time runs against him. He might go up for a morning meeting with the intention of spending the rest of the day there, but invariably finds himself dashing back to something else.

In these circumstances, the quality of Ed's interactions is vital. He needs to get the most from every conversation, and this means phrasing his questions carefully and concentrating hard on what people tell him, especially on what they're telling him when they're not, overtly, telling him something. With time at a premium he needs to get to the point, and this means sussing out where a conversation is going and moving it on.

ing. So you need to test them out, and you must always be prepared to change your mind. You must always keep an open mind.

Most of us like to think of ourselves as open-minded, but the fact is that we don't like changing our minds. Once we have come to a particular view of something that view tends to stick, even if new evidence goes against it. This is understandable. We are surrounded by information that is confusing and uncertain and couldn't possibly keep it all 'on hold', so speak. We have to make sense of things in order to act, to get on with life, and so to some extent the making sense of things – finding a story that more or less fits the information – is more important in practice than what sense we make of them. Putting an interpretation on the information we've gathered simplifies things and reduces our feeling of uncertainty. We are naturally reluctant to complicate them again, and create more uncertainty, by questioning that interpretation.

Having come to a particular view of things, then, we stick with it, perhaps changing it incrementally, at the edges, if that easily accommodates any new information, but not changing it fundamentally. Instead of changing the story to fit the evidence, we interpret the evidence to fit the story. Or if we can't do that, we dismiss the evidence as being anomalous or unrepresentative. Or we just blind ourselves to it and pretend it's not there. You can see this process in operation all the time, at work, at home or in the public sphere. We all despair at how other people seem fixed in their mindsets, even when the information clearly calls for a change of mind. Yet we all do the same ourselves.

If you want to be an effective manager, you need to guard against this tendency, and the only way to do it is to consciously force yourself to keep an open mind. You have to draw conclusions and work with them, or else you would get nothing done, but try and treat those conclusions as provisional. Consciously look, in your inquisitiveness, for information that might throw doubt on them. Work out the key assumptions on which your managerial approach is based – assumptions about your staff, about your objectives and about the environment in which you are operating – and periodically review those against any new information you might have gathered.

And don't worry about changing your mind! Don't keep changing it. If you keep changing your mind from day to day, you won't make any progress and you'll hopelessly confuse your staff. Any practical conclusion or course of action has to be robust enough to cope with small changes in circumstances and, as we shall see later, stability in the directions you set for your team is an important part of effective management. But the world changes. If circumstances change significantly, there is evidence of this happening and you're suitably inquisitive, the information available to you will change accordingly, and there will come a point where you have to revisit your conclusions and change your course of action. As the great and unusually open-minded economist (economists are not usually open-minded) John Maynard Keynes once said, in response to a criticism that he'd changed his policy advice: 'When my information changes, I alter my conclusions. What do you do, Sir?' Should you stick with a conclusion when the evidence no longer supports it? Of course not – but it takes a disciplined mind to avoid doing so.

17 LEARN TO SEE THE WORLD
AS OTHER PEOPLE SEE IT

One of the features of the way we interpret information is that it is very personal. We all have a tendency to assume that the way we see things is more or less the way they are, and we all struggle to understand how other people can possibly see them so differently. How can anyone possibly believe in all that religious stuff? How can anyone possibly doubt it? Surely it's obvious that immigrants are a drain on the country? How can people not understand that they are net contributors? The fact is that different people see things differently, and while some of these differences can be resolved by debate, others can't. Think about parents arguing with their teenage children. We've all been teenagers and we all know that we were right. Many of us have been parents too and are convinced that we were right then too. At the end of the day, no person's view is privileged, and certainly not mine or yours.

This is a general observation and it applies to work as much as to anything else. Think of how a particular business problem would be viewed by an accountant, a marketer or a production engineer. Their analyses would be quite different. Or think of how a change in employment conditions might be viewed by a chief executive and a shop steward, or how a particular welfare provision might be viewed by a civil servant and a politician. Their viewpoints will differ and the views they get from those viewpoints will naturally differ too.

Just as important, Jack may see things quite differently from Jill, even if they share very similar backgrounds, experiences and professional training. We all make assumptions about how the world works, and if one person assumes people to be fundamentally self-serving, say, while another assumes them to fundamentally altruistic and cooperative, they will put completely different interpretations on things.

Most important of all, your view, like any view, will always be partial, selective and biased in all sorts of ways. You will inevitably miss things that other people will see, and interpret what you do see in ways that are quite wide of the mark – the 'mark' in this case being not some complete and probably unknowable truth, but what is most important about the situation now. And even when you see what somebody else sees, you need to understand how they see it.

There is a famous poem by Stevie Smith in which a man seen in the waves laments, 'I was much further out than you thought/ And not waving but drowning'. If one of your staff is drowning not waving, you need to know, either by seeing things from their perspective or by taking on board what some other observer, more sensitive to the particular problem, can see. If you see a situation as threatening and someone else sees it as an opportunity – or vice versa – you need to know. One person's efficiency saving is another's health and safety risk: you need to see both sides.

To manage well you need to learn to put yourself in somebody else's position, see the things that they see and see those things as they see them. There is no special skill involved here, though one of the techniques discussed in Chapter 7 ('soft systems' methodology') may sometimes help. You just need to make a determined effort and to keep reminding yourself that what you take for objective knowledge is probably just your own idiosyncratic point of view. So test it out on other people and, if they don't see things as you do, don't just assume that the fault lies with them. The people you encounter at work are not generally stupid. They are not deaf and blind. And they are not fantasists: if they see things it is probably because those things are there to be seen, and if they interpret them in a certain way, it is because they have reasons of some kind to do so. They are no doubt blinkered and prejudiced, but so are you, and the difference is simply that they are prejudiced in different ways.

18 LISTEN VERY CAREFULLY, EVEN WHEN YOU ARE TALKING

It is hard to over-estimate the importance of listening and, where appropriate, of watching. The whole point of being available and being inquisitive is to listen to what people have to say. And you can only see the world as other people see it, and understand where they're coming from, if you listen carefully, not only to what they are saying but also to what they're not saying, and to what they are 'really' saying.

As we've already noted, some people find it very difficult to listen at all. They seem to be much more interested in the sound of their own voice and in their own words of wisdom than in anyone else's. Other people listen to the words, but reinterpret them to fit in with their own preconceptions. Indeed most of us do this to some extent. We jump from the evidence of what people are saying – their words and sentences – to conclusions about what they mean or what they are thinking.

These conclusions are often hypothetical and quite unwarranted. In an ordinary social setting, when the main aim is just to enjoy or get through a conversation, this might not matter too much. Sometimes it helps to go along as if we are in agreement, or at least understand each other, even when we're not. Sometimes our misunderstandings generate argument and liven everything up. In any serious context, however, where the point of listening is to understand and learn, the habit of imposing our own interpretations on what people say is distinctly counter-productive and potentially harmful.

So your inquisitiveness has to go beyond just getting an answer. You have to understand what people mean by the answers they give. You have to ask how these answers have been tailored to you as the questioner. You have to understand, as far as you can, what people might be thinking but not saying, what they might be leaving out and why. You have to be inquisitive through and through. So you carefully watch people's expressions and body language. You listen carefully to their phrasing and choice of words. You listen carefully to their silences and hesitations.

All of this applies not only when you are questioning someone, but even when you are the one doing the talking. The great Jewish philosopher, Martin Buber, once observed that, as all the best teachers know, the most important part of lecturing is listening. Teachers are there to convey information and to prompt questioning, but they are also there, more fundamentally, to help people grow and develop. Buber's comment was associated with a case in which a student in his class was crying out for help and he didn't realize it. But the advice also holds on a more prosaic level. The point of teaching is to communicate and that only happens when the person you are teaching receives the intended communication. Teachers can't know if they're getting their messages across unless they are constantly watching and listening, even as they talk, to how the students are responding to what they say.

The same applies in any management situation, not just when you are mentoring someone, but when you are instructing them, informing them or just engaging with them informally. Talking to someone is not communicating with them. It is only the beginning of a communication and, if you are to complete the job, you also have to watch and listen to their responses, or to their lack of response, and then respond yourself to that. The process is open-ended because there'll always be a gap between what is going on in your mind as you seek to communicate and what is going on in theirs as a result of the communication. But even if you can never close this gap, it helps a lot if you can narrow it.

Buber's own example is also something you should keep in mind. Everybody goes through difficult times and some people sometimes go through extremely difficult times. The problems may be personal and nothing to do with work. But as somebody's manager, you are an important person in their life and this gives you a responsibility that goes beyond their work. Most of the time you will not want to get involved in their problems, but you will want to be aware of them, to take account of them and not exacerbate them, and to do what you can to see that the person gets help if it is needed. If somebody's words give no obvious cause for concern but you hear something about the way they are being said, that suggests they are putting a brave face on things, that they are really suffering, let us

---

Example 11: Active Listening

We noted in the last example how Melanie's inquisitiveness, and her encouragement of inquisitiveness in her nurses, enables her both to identify potential problems and to facilitate the contacts needed to solve them. By listening carefully, by active listening, she can also do more than this. Many organizations are made up of people from different backgrounds and different specialties who don't communicate easily with each other and struggle to see things from each other's perspectives. Hospitals are a prime example of this, as the perspectives of administrators, clinicians, nursing and support staff are all very different. Interacting as she has to with all these groups, Melanie is perfectly placed to bridge the gaps between them. Every junior or middle manager has to be, among other things, an interpreter, putting directions from above in terms her staff can understand and expressing staff concerns in terms her superiors can understand. In Melanie's case, she finds herself interpreting across, as well as up and down, using her interactions to see things from different perspectives and linking those perspectives together. She can't quite think like a consultant doctor, let alone like a hospital administrator, but she can get part of the way there and can act as a bridge between them, helping them get their points across and avoiding misunderstandings.

In the very different context of an engineering firm, Ed shares this ability. He doesn't have Melanie's natural empathy but over many years as a manager he's developed the skill of bringing

---

say, from serious and undiagnosed depression; don't just let things drift on from bad to worse: do something.

19 EVEN LISTEN TO THE RUMOURS, BUT DON'T BELIEVE THEM!

If you make yourself available, chat to people informally and keep your ears open, one of the things you will probably hear quite a lot of is gossip. Some of this will be personal and have little to do with work, but much of it will be work-related. You will hear a lot, for example, about decisions that have supposedly been taken but not formally announced. You will hear about appointments that will

---

people who think very differently into a productive conversation. Sometimes this entails acting as an interpreter in meetings involving different functions – sales and product development, for example, or accounting and manufacturing. Sometimes it entails acting as a messenger-translator, as he does between the subsidiary and the headquarters, representing each to the other in the other's language. He's never sure quite how effective he is at this. People will always say they've got the message, whether they have or not. But something gets across, and enough to keep things working.

When it comes to gossip, Ed and Melanie have different attitudes. Melanie enjoys the gossip of the hospital and hears an awful lot of it, but she never puts any store by it. There's far too much to analyse; most of it is not, anyway, relevant to doing her job; and when it is, it's utterly unreliable. Ed hears less gossip. Indeed, if he wasn't so inquisitive, he'd probably not hear any. And most of what he hears he doesn't believe. But it's sometimes the source of a good laugh, and several times over the years it's alerted him to problems brewing in the company, and enabled him to nip them in the bud. One time, for example, the whole factory was about to go on strike on the basis of a completely false rumour. Another time a policy imposed by head office, that had seemed on the face of it quite innocuous to him, had caused deep resentment in one of his sections, and by the time he picked up the gossip, several first-rate staff were on the point of moving to another firm. Had they come to him with their concerns, of course, he could have allayed them. But sometimes people don't.

'almost certainly' be made, about redundancies or sackings that are in the offing, and about impending changes in rules and procedures. You will hear that senior manager X has had an argument with worker Y, that Z has been denied compassionate leave and that your office is to be relocated to the other side of town or to the other end of the country. You will hear all sorts of conspiracy theories and you will be astonishingly well-informed about the future, as well as the past.

Much of this gossip will be based on rumours, some of which will be very plausible. Others will be quite preposterous, but plausible enough to the gossip-mongers to cause alarm and be taken seriously. Some of them may be soundly based: news does leak out, through indiscretion or conversations overheard. If told something in strict confidence ('don't tell anyone'), most people will assume, if it's a work matter, that telling their spouses is somehow OK. The spouses then talk to their friends or relations and, by one route or another, the information finds its way back into the organization, often with quite astonishing speed. The great majority of rumours, however, are unfounded. Sometimes they are spread maliciously. Sometimes what starts out as a good joke gets taken seriously. Sometimes a rumour starts out by being quite accurate, but through a process of Chinese whispers and successive re-interpretations, as people tailor communications to their own preconceptions, it gets so distorted as to become quite fantastical.

Some managers prefer to ignore rumours completely. So long as you remember that they are just rumours, however, they always tell you something. If nothing else, they tell you about people's prejudices and preconceptions, about what they are frightened of and about what they are suspicious of. What you shouldn't do is take them for fact. You also need to be careful how you respond to them. Sometimes, if they are doing a lot of damage, you may have to squash them. If they are based on attitudes or prejudices that you are trying to change, you can use them as an opportunity to make those explicit and challenge people. But if you make a habit of trying to squash rumours whenever they arise, people will start using you as a check on whether or not they are true, and you don't want to get into that position.

20 DON'T PANIC – TAKE YOUR TIME, CONSULT AND THINK BEFORE YOU ACT

We have so far focused more on the general art of being a manager than on the specific tasks that managers have to execute. This is important precisely because it is not written down anywhere. It is not in the job description, yet it is the core of the job. But managers do, obviously, have to do things. As a manager you will have to complete a variety of more or less routine administrative tasks. You will have to make decisions. And you will have to make plans. So how should you approach these?

Let's begin with those urgent decisions that arise when something happens that is out of the normal routine – a glitch, a crisis, an accident, a delivery strike, a machine breaking down, a process breaking down, a person breaking down, whatever – and it falls to you, as a manager, to decide what to do.

We all react in different ways to this kind of situation. Some people's heads seem to be much clearer in a crisis, while other people's are much more muddled. Some move instinctively to action, in direct response to events. They are at their best when they don't have to think, only to act. Others freeze or need time to internalize what is going on and get to grips with it. But crises themselves vary. There are situations in which immediate action is essential: a building on fire or a serious accident. Here what matters is that someone takes control and prevents panic. As a manager you should know who in your unit can be trusted in such circumstances to keep cool and to keep a clear head. If you are the person on the scene with the greatest authority, you should either take control yourself or immediately mandate someone else to do so, if they will do it better.

Most management crises, however, are not at all like this. They may call for prompt action but they rarely call for immediate action, and the action they call for is much less obvious. It is not just a question of getting people out of a building quickly, safely and in an orderly fashion, or calling an ambulance and giving first aid, but of something much more complex. Various actions may need to be taken and instructions given. Mistakes may have to be identified and addressed. Some people may have to be placated, others informed and so on. And in these much more typical situations, acting too quickly can be just as harmful as acting too slowly. The basic rule, 'Don't panic', still applies, but there is generally time to think things through and there are generally things to be thought through.

This need not take long. Very often the decision you would take after an hour's reflection (even an hour's subconscious reflection, while you get on with other things) will be quite different from that you would take immediately, and much better. It will be a thoughtful decision, not a knee-jerk reaction. Giving yourself twenty-four hours to sleep on a problem, perhaps by taking some kind of holding action meanwhile, will almost always result in an even better decision.

Giving yourself this little bit of extra time also has two other significant benefits. First, it enables you to consult with other people: with your boss, with other managers, with people in the unit whose judgement you trust. Your immediate thoughts in response to a problem will generally be about how to deal with it yourself, not about who might help you to deal with it better; but, if you give yourself time to think about the problem, you will naturally take a broader view and ask what other people might think. If you have to take some kind of holding action, moreover, this in itself will provide an opportunity for consultation. Just telling people (your own manager, your staff) that you haven't yet decided what to do invites discussion, which could well be invaluable.

Second, it allows you to choose your words with care. If you plunge straight into action, you might well find that, even if the actions are appropriate, the messages you convey in the process are not. Your focus will be on immediate outcomes and you might easily let your annoyance show, upset people or blame them prematurely. You may also lose any potential learning benefit from the incident. Much better to work out carefully not only the actions needed, but also the story accompanying them, so as to minimize any harm done and to use the situation as productively as possible.

Having said all this, you shouldn't give yourself too much time! When told that someone thought three times before acting, Confucius is reported to have commented, 'Twice is enough'. And so it is. The first time you won't think through it properly, but by the third time you will be doubting your own judgements and losing your clarity. So stop and think, but when you've thought it through and consulted and worked out what to say, stop thinking and act.

21 WHEN DECISIONS DON'T MATTER, TAKE THEM QUICKLY

Most managerial decisions aren't made under crisis conditions. You will have time to make them and the freedom to choose how you go about making them: whether you simply follow your own judgement, whether you consult people first and then act, or whether you set up some sort of decision-making machinery. The choice will partly depend upon the culture of the organization and its formal procedural structures. But you will generally have some degree of freedom, and different managers within the organization will typically proceed in different ways. So how should you proceed?

When it comes to decision-making, you have two duties as a manager. One is to ensure that decisions are made, when called for, in a timely and efficient manner. The other is to ensure that the right decisions are made and that their consequences are well managed. These duties can easily conflict, so you have to take some care over how you balance them and adopt different tactics in different situations.

Some managerial decisions are really not very important. Whether choosing equipment or suppliers, allocating offices, dividing up duties, scheduling meetings or rotas, you may have two or three options, none of which is significantly better or worse than the others. Of course the people affected will have their own personal preferences, and you should always ask them what these are (why not – you may be able to please everybody). But what matters most is that a decision is taken so that everyone can get on with life, and whichever choice you make, it will soon be forgotten or taken for granted.

In these cases, just make a decision, quickly and without fuss. People can spend hours or days arguing and agonizing over whether the carpet should be a bluish green or a greenish blue. At the end of the day it probably doesn't matter, and their time and energy would be much better spent getting on with other things. So would yours.

Some of these decisions, while trivial in themselves, may be very important to the people concerned. Offices and desks, for example, always seem to be quite extraordinarily important to people, even though they very quickly get used to whatever they are allocated. Once you allow people to go beyond stating their preferences, however, to pleading their cases, things quickly get out of hand. So just decide quickly, if necessary by some kind of random choice.

Another example might be if two people have had some kind of misunderstanding. Suppose, for example, that each was expecting to take Friday off but one of them has to be at work, that both have made arrangements and each one is strongly convinced that the fault lies with the other. If the reality of the situation is fairly clear-cut, your decision will be easy, but if you have no way of telling what has happened, your decision should still be easy. Sorry, you say, I have to make a call and it's this. Be fair, but be decisive. And don't waste too much effort over it.

Some organizations use committees to make most of their decisions, so that even quite trivial decisions have to go through a formal process of proposal, circulation, discussion and committee approval. If such a system is to work efficiently, however, the same guidelines apply. Chairing a committee is an art in itself and beyond the scope of this book, but most of the general advice given here, about how you behave and how you treat people, carries over. In the case of decision-making, your job as a chairman is to make sure that the important decisions are fully discussed and that the committee's time isn't wasted on the trivial or uncontentious ones. With expert chairing, 90 per cent of the business of a typical committee can be dispatched in seconds, with all sorts of benefits. Not only is plenty of time left for the things that matter, but the committee members also get into the habit of speaking only when they have something significant to contribute, and not offering their opinions, at length, on anything and everything, which they might tend to under a less efficient chair.

22 WHEN DECISIONS DO MATTER, GIVE EVERYONE A VOICE

While some decisions don't really matter, others matter a lot. In those cases, you should not only allow time for the decision process, but also make sure that, within the established procedures of the organization, everybody with something to contribute gets the chance to contribute.

Whom you involve in a decision will, of course, depend on what is being decided. In the case of appointing to a job vacancy, for example, you will generally have some kind of appointments' committee with members chosen for their relevant knowledge, their experience and their ability to look at things objectively. (It is always a good idea, whether or not the organization requires it, to involve someone from another part of the organization.) You will no doubt have your own view on whom to appoint, but always listen carefully to other views and the reasons for them, even if you have the final say. You should also solicit informal impressions from some of the people with whom the appointee will work. These may include very personal reactions that you will wish to discount, but they may well include valuable observations, made outside the very artificial setting of a formal interview.

Another kind of decision that is almost always important is a decision on promotions. Getting or failing to get a promotion is obviously very important to the person concerned, but these decisions also send strong messages about the qualities that are valued in the organization. Here, consulting explicitly with an applicant's peers will not normally be appropriate, but you will still want to know something about what their views are. And even more than in the case of a new appointment, you will want to consider a variety of opinions, both to get the decision right and to ensure that it is made fairly, and is not just a reflection of your own, or perhaps your own boss's, prejudices.

Some decisions are important because they significantly affect the future of the unit. You may be trying to decide on a strategy for taking a business forward, for example, on a major investment in buildings, plant or machinery, on a new organizational structure or on measures to recover from a sustained drop in performance. Decisions of this kind are likely to take time. You may need to commission some serious analysis and you will want to solicit the views of a wide range of players: the people in your unit, people elsewhere in the organization (if appropriate) and a variety of external stakeholders. These might include key customers, suppliers, trade unions, shareholders, local communities, NGOs and so on – the list will depend on the situation.

Your criteria here are essentially twofold. You should consult with people who make a constructive contribution, whether in the form of their knowledge and experience or in the form of their own plans and intentions. And you should consult with people when it would be harmful not to consult with them, either because they have a valid interest and should be consulted, as a matter of justice or fairness, or because of the damage that might result if they were ignored.

Once again, if the decision is to be made by committee, the same general rules apply. First, commission any necessary analysis or surveys. Then make sure that everybody with a stake in the issue is represented on the committee, either through a spokesperson or through a written submission. Then, when the committee comes to its deliberations, make sure that every voice is not just heard, but actively listened to. The whole process may feel laborious but, by following the process, you will both reach a better decision and gain acceptance, however reluctantly, for that decision. If no-one can say that their views weren't properly considered, the grounds for objection are greatly reduced.

Not every decision can be easily classified as being important or unimportant. There will inevitably be borderline cases, including issues that look unimportant to you but turn out to be important, for very good reasons, to other people. So you must always be prepared to backtrack and reconsider, if necessary. If chairing a committee you may run quickly through the unimportant business, but you must listen carefully and watch people's reactions as you do so. Similarly, in other contexts. Don't be afraid to say, 'Sorry, I thought that was uncontentious, but maybe I was wrong. Let's

Example 12: Decisions, Decisions

When it comes to making decisions, two things above all characterize the different situations our managers find themselves in. The first is psychology. Some people are naturally more decisive than others. The second is organizational culture. Some organizations are biased towards executive decision-making, others towards consultation and consensus.

In the case of Rick's restaurant, most of the decision-making comes down to him. The style and character of the place are dictated by the owner, but everything else is up to Rick. Unfortunately, Rick himself is naturally indecisive. Indeed, if he were more decisive he would probably be running his own restaurant by now and not someone else's – opportunities have arisen on several occasions, but by the time he's made up his mind to go for them, the opportunities have passed. In the restaurant, his inclination is always to consult with his staff and to build up a picture of the arguments for and against any action. On straightforward, day-to-day issues, this works quite well. In a small organization, consultation is quick and easy, and knowing his weakness he has publicly committed himself to fast decisions. He still sometimes prevaricates, but when he does so, the stock question, 'What's the answer, boss?', will bring an answer. When it comes to the difficult questions, however, the more he does this, the more balanced the arguments seem to become and the harder the decision.

A current challenge has arisen after a change in the menus, followed, a couple of months later, by a modest but significant and growing decline in turnover. People are actually spending more, but there are fewer of them. The chef is strongly committed to the new dishes, and they are good: he can be proud of them. But either they don't appeal to the customers who are attracted to the restaurant's style and ambience, or something else, completely unrelated, is causing the decline. Or perhaps there is just a period of adjustment and over time trade will pick up again, with numbers returning to normal and a higher spend. But there is no sign of that yet, the losses are mounting and there is a danger that the old customers will be lost for good and the lower numbers will themselves make the place less attractive, that it will lose its buzz.

Rick has consulted with everyone. The kitchens are strongly for sticking. The owner seems to be for going back to the old menus but insists that Rick take the decision (and the blame!).

The front-of-house staff, whose views he particularly values on account of their close customer contacts, are divided. Rick is half tempted to toss a coin, but that would be ducking out. The fact is he has to make a decision, and it is already overdue.

Meanwhile, in another world altogether, Polly, the primary head, also faces difficult decisions. When it comes to strategic or longer term decisions, she is effectively working in a bureaucratic context. The biggest decisions are taken for her, by government or the local authority, and the next layer down have to be approved both by the local authority and by the school governors. This involves a cumbersome process of formal proposals and supporting paperwork, and a decision process in which educational and political objectives get mixed up and played against each other.

When it comes to the day-to-day running of the school, Polly has a relatively free hand. She can take decisions off her own bat and she's psychologically inclined to do that. Give her a problem and her instinct is to decide there and then what to do about it. She has learnt, however, to restrain herself.

A recent issue is fairly typical. The first Polly knew of it was when a young assistant teacher, Annie, came to her at the end of the day complaining that her class teacher, Carrie, had used unnecessary force in restraining a five-year-old boy, Fred, after Fred had hit another child, Fanny. Apparently the hit was accidental and Fred was restrained as he tried to cuddle Fanny in apology. The next morning, Polly had Carrie in her office in tears, having been verbally abused and threatened by Fanny's mother. And later in the day she had Fanny's mother in her office complaining that Fanny had been violently assaulted by Fred, that this wasn't the first time and that Carrie had tried to pass it off as an accident; and demanding that Fred be excluded, or at least moved to a parallel class forthwith, immediately.

Polly knew, or at least thought she knew, what had happened, and what she had to do about it, both in terms of immediate action and in terms of the procedures that would have to be followed subsequently. But she also knew somewhere in the back of her mind that she could possibly be wrong and that it was very important to be right. And that meant calming everybody down, making some more inquiries and doing nothing hasty. She had to act, and she had to act within days, but if she could give herself a couple of days then everyone might benefit.

discuss it.' You won't always get these things right, but it's much better to get nine out of ten right and admit that you're wrong the tenth time, than it is to impose your judgement every time, or to refrain from any judgement at all.

23 ROUTINE ADMINISTRATION MATTERS – DO IT CONSCIENTIOUSLY AND EFFICIENTLY

We often think of managers as being primarily decision-makers, and so in a sense they are. If there were no decisions to be made, there would be no need to have people with the authority and status of managers. But managers are also form-fillers, report-writers, appraisers, expenditure authorizers, compliance officers and committee fodder. They are, in other words, routine administrators.

It is easy to get frustrated by these demands and to underestimate their importance. They take up a lot of time. They are often tedious. They rarely seem to require any great skill. They don't always seem to achieve anything. The temptation is to get them out of the way as quickly as possible: to skip through the committee papers, to sign things without checking carefully on what you are signing, to knock off reports as quickly as you can; or else to put them off or to avoid them altogether. Surely this form doesn't really have to be in by the date specified? It won't matter if I miss that meeting.

These temptations are quite understandable but the administration is there for a reason. Organizations don't organize themselves. They need systems for controlling what has to be controlled, for getting information where it is needed, when it is needed and for coordinating their multiple, often complex activities. Even simple organizations, like owner-managed businesses, small charities or professional partnerships, need to conform to legal and regulatory requirements and to exercise due diligence. It's a bit like personal administration, like filling in a tax return or renewing a parking permit. This is equally tedious, but our complex society couldn't function without it.

Many routine administrative tasks also impact on other people, and failure to do them promptly and conscientiously can impact quite seriously. So long as you don't process an expenses claim, the claimant will be out of pocket. If you don't prepare a case for promotion, or if you do it without the often time-consuming care and attention it needs, somebody may be denied promotion, even though they thoroughly deserve it. If you don't write your reports carefully and submit them on time, or if you don't turn up to meetings, managers elsewhere in the organization will be deprived of the information they need. Their judgement will suffer and their staff will bear the consequences. If you don't carefully check a risk assessment document, you will fail to notice any errors or oversights, and your staff will be exposed to unnecessary risk. And so on.

These tasks fall on managers for two reasons. First, managers are paid to be responsible and accountable, and they are chosen, amongst other things, for their responsibility. Even though many administrative tasks are not highly skilled, they do entail considerable responsibility. You couldn't ask junior members of staff, paid according to their more limited skills, to take this level of responsibility for the welfare of others and for the smooth functioning of the organization as a whole. Second, because of their pivotal role as communicators and gatekeepers, managers have the information needed. Only managers, well-informed about both their own units and the needs of the organization as a whole, have the information needed to write the reports, to contribute to the committee discussions and to confirm the accuracy of other people's claims. Routine as it may seem, most of the administration that managers undertake just can't be delegated.

So the administration has to be done. And since you have to do it, you might as well enjoy it. You will certainly find life more enjoyable if you can go to bed knowing that you have done the things that people rely on you to do. And once you look at administration in the right way – not, perhaps as an adventure exactly, but as a pleasant enough pastime and not just an annoyance or inconvenience – it can actually be very enjoyable. There is a lot of pleasure to be had in doing any task well and in getting it satisfactorily completed, even if the task is routine. After all, many people take pleasure in mowing their lawns or weeding their flowerbeds, in DIY, in cooking and even in ironing. There is great pleasure to be had in producing a document that people find helpful or in contributing to a committee when it reaches a satisfactory consensus. And there is an even greater pleasure to be had in securing a bonus or promotion for someone who really deserves it.

24 ROUTINE ADMINISTRATION ISN'T ALL THAT MATTERS – DON'T LET IT DROWN YOU

The importance of routine administration and the rewards to be gained from doing it conscientiously should never be underestimated. But nor should the dangers of getting submerged. For every

Example 13: Routine Administration

Administration weighs much more heavily on some of our managers than on others. For Rick and Brad, the main administrative challenge is just that of running a small business, making sure that the bills get paid on time, that health and safety regulations are observed and so on. The red tape involved with such businesses has grown over time. Rick's restaurant is subject to a host of fire, safety and hygiene regulations, requiring regular assessments and scrupulous monitoring and record-keeping. Brad's vans have to be licensed to carry waste oil and other products. Providing they keep on top of things, however, the time commitment is manageable. The problem is keeping on top of them. The danger is that with administration always having to be fitted in around other things, and never the top priority, things can easily get put aside and then forgotten, so that deadlines pass. Or else things get done at the last minute, in a desperate hurry, so that mistakes are made.

The managers with the heaviest administrative loads are Belle, the bank manager, Polly, the head teacher, and Melanie, the hospital matron. For Belle, administration is a large part of her job. Even when she's doing other things, like coaching her staff or making decisions, it's usually within an administrative framework. Indeed, in other contexts or in other historical time periods she would have been called an administrator, not a manager. She can't skip or neglect administrative tasks: she is expected to give them all her attention and she is assessed on how accurately and how thoroughly she does them; but her job description allows for this. She isn't tempted to skip or neglect them, because they don't get pushed out of the way by other tasks.

manager who neglects it, there is another who drowns in it and who ends up without either the time or the energy to do the other important things, like making decisions and mentoring staff.

This is always a danger, because while routine administration is necessary, it has an inbuilt tendency to expand. Sixty years ago the distinguished naval historian and humourist, Cyril Northcote Parkinson, proposed the first version of what has come to be known as Parkinson's Law: that bureaucratic work expands to fill the time available for its completion. Parkinson's particular focus was on

For Polly and Melanie things are more difficult. Being a school head should not really be the same as being an administrator. Polly has no administrative training, and what matters to her – the reasons she's in the job – are teaching and developing young children. But the red tape associated with running a school has grown massively in recent years and, like most heads, Polly can be overwhelmed by it. Together with trouble-shooting and the time she insists on spending in the classroom, necessarily if she is to know her staff and exercise her responsibility for the children, it takes up all her working week and more, leaving little time for anything else, be it leadership, coaching or planning for the future. But it has to be done and it has to be done properly.

The other manager weighed under by inescapable administration is Melanie, the matron. The British National Health Service is one of the largest organizations in the world, eclipsed only by the Chinese Communist Party and the Indian Railways, and like most massive organizations, it is massively bureaucratic. Division into free-standing operating units, like the Foundation Trust of which Melanie's hospital is a part, has just added extra layers of administration and administrative procedures. Fortunately, Melanie has few responsibilities for planning and doesn't carry the level of responsibility generally that Polly has as a school head. She can concentrate more easily on the administrative side, and she's learnt that by keeping on top of it and doing it efficiently, she can make her life, and the lives of her colleagues and staff, a lot easier. But she still faces a big challenge in finding the time to reflect on all the information she absorbs so as to put it to productive use.

the British Civil Service and, especially, the Colonial Office in the days of a shrinking empire, which grew larger and larger the fewer colonies it had to administer. In that context, the desire of managers to increase the number of their subordinates and the tendency of officials to make work for each other, combined to cause a steady growth in both administrative tasks and staff numbers. Left to itself, he suggested, any bureaucracy would grow by between 5 per cent and 7 per cent a year. This effect can be seen in all kinds of organizations, especially when they are trying to rationalize.

Replace three modestly paid middle managers by one highly paid supremo and the supremo will soon need four assistants, each paid more than the original managers. But other forces are at work too, and in many organizations the tasks multiply relentlessly without any extra staff to do them. It is always easier to add in a new administrative requirement than to cut out an old one, especially in an age of ever-increasing scrutiny and regulation.

The consequence is that routine administration threatens to take over a manager's job completely, leaving no time for anything else. Diligent managers can all too easily find that their days (and possibly their evenings too) are filled with necessary duties, and that they have neither the time nor the energy to mentor their staff or to engage with the strategy and direction of their units, never mind to make themselves available or to engage in informal communications or networks. Like the Red Queen in *Alice Through the Looking Glass* they have to keep running hard to stay in the same place, and never manage to move forwards.

So while you have to be conscientious about performing your administrative duties, you also have to keep them under control. This is partly just a question of efficient working. One of the 'corollaries' of Parkinson's Law proposed by other writers is that work contracts to fit the time available, and with a disciplined approach to this aspect of your work, you will find that, to some extent, this is true. It is largely a question of attitude. Some of the managers who drown in administration are simply out of their depth. Consciously or unconsciously, they are trying to avoid other tasks, perhaps because they find them too difficult or too challenging. They stay under water because they don't want to face up to what's on the surface. But others flounder because they don't give the task enough concentration and attention. They find swimming boring, so they don't swim properly and sink. If you approach routine administration expecting it to be a trial and a bore, you won't concentrate on it properly and it will take much longer than it should do. If you approach it more positively and give it your full attention, you will find that your head is much clearer and you get through things much more quickly as a result.

There will be times, of course, when even with an efficient approach and the right attitude, the administrative requirements simply get too much and something has to give. Then you have to prioritize. Perhaps they can do without you at that meeting, if the other people are competent and trustworthy. Perhaps that deadline can be extended, so long as people know that your report is coming, and exactly when it is coming. But that other report is needed on time and that personal reference not only needs to be sent off, but needs to be very carefully drafted.

As a manager you will always have competing demands on your attention. You will always have to prioritize. The important things are that you choose your priorities for good reasons and not just for your personal convenience, and that you take account of the consequences for other people of your not doing things or delaying doing them.

25 MAKE TIME REGULARLY TO THINK AND TO REFLECT

Of all the things that are apt to get crowded out by routine administration, the most likely to suffer is thinking – especially hard, concentrated thinking about difficult or complex issues; deep, reflective thinking about ethical and motivational issues; and creative, imaginative thinking about how to do things differently and better.

Many of the guidelines suggested above call for thinking of these kinds. You will need to think hard about costs and value added, how the organization works, performance and performance measures, and the environment in which you are operating. You will need to think creatively about how to add more value, and how and where to find things out. You will need to think reflectively about trust and respect, about how best to deal with mistakes or personality clashes, and about how best to help your staff learn and develop. If you are to learn to see things as other people see them, you will need to combine hard thinking with imagination and reflection.

The need for time to think and reflect will become even more apparent when we look at some of the more difficult challenges you might face: engaging strategically with the future, leading people through change and maintaining your ethical awareness. The question is, though, when and where are you going to find it? The days when managers could shut themselves up in their offices and think through their problems in peace have long since gone. Research into how managers spend their time shows that the entire working day (and it is typically a long working day) is spent in meetings, on the phone, reading and responding to emails, or in routine administrative tasks, like checking and signing off forms. The routine administration that calls for more prolonged attention, like reading and writing reports or preparing budgets, is often done at home or on the train or plane. If more serious thinking is done at all, it is in the car, in the bath or on holiday.

This is not a recipe for success or even for job satisfaction. It is often said that the secret of combining a busy job with a happy family life is to give the family 'quality time', and that is exactly what you need here. You don't need much time – no more, perhaps, than an hour a week on a regular basis, more when you have a major issue to deal with. But you do need quality time, time in which you can think seriously and concentrate effectively without interruption and without distractions.

It is very helpful to have a cue of some kind. The Islamic religion requires everybody to pray five times a day and in Islamic firms and other organizations this is built into the working day. Prayer time, and the physical accoutrements that accompany it, acts as a sharp cut-off between one way of thinking and another. Muslim managers will typically shift from an active to a reflective mode and this at least helps them to stay ethically aware, though a prayerful mode is not well-suited to hard, concentrated thinking about business problems. In the more leisured times of the 1950s and 1960s, managers in large bureaucratic corporations would allocate a regular time slot for thinking at work in much the same way as they allocated a regular time slot for relaxing with a gin and tonic when they got home. That is virtually impossible nowadays, but you can still use cues and props to help you switch modes quickly. A simple cup of tea, if combined with fifteen or twenty minutes solitude (five minutes to change gear, ten or fifteen minutes to think), might be enough to do the trick.

But can you find even twenty minutes? Yes, you can. And the reason is that a change is as good as a rest. When we work as hard as managers typically do, we don't work very efficiently, and the longer we work without a break of some kind, the less efficient we get. A thinking interlude, if you can get it right, works a bit like a catnap or a meditation break. It breaks the unproductive chains of routine thoughts going round and round getting nowhere, brings your brain back under control and enables you to start afresh. The twenty minutes lost will soon be made up.

Sometimes, of course, you can't find the twenty minutes, even with the best will in the world and even though it would pay dividends. And sometimes your brain is so muddled up and whirring round that you simply can't get it in order without a much more prolonged break. At times like that you may have to leave your quality thinking to the weekends or holidays, but the 'quality' rule still applies. Find time regularly to think – don't keep putting it off. And discipline yourself. If you're not thinking clearly, don't keep on wading through treacle and neglecting what you should be doing at the weekend or on holiday. Stop, do something else, then start again. If you can keep your discipline, you'll get there eventually.

26 PLAN AHEAD, BUT REALISTICALLY

One of the things for which you will want quality thinking time is planning ahead. This could address a range of issues. You might need to plan a strategy for building or sustaining a business, for marketing a new product, or for responding to changing customer or client needs. Or you might need to plan out how you will implement, in your unit, a strategy drawn up by others. You might need to undertake some kind of succession planning. You might be planning a process of financial or operational reviews. You might just be planning your own routine administrative work around a calendar of formal deadlines, or planning the routine administration of your staff.

Planning ahead for these kinds of things is important for two reasons. First, there are things that need to be done, including both routine activities and routinized responses to recurrent or predictably possible events, and they won't get done if they're not planned in advance. People will do what is on the agenda or in the calendar (i.e. what has already been planned), and they will do what they can to cope with events as they happen, but they are unlikely to do anything else.

Second, without planning you risk being entirely at the mercy of events. If you have plans for meeting a range of different circumstances or responding to a range of possible events, you have some chance of being in control when they arise. Without planning, you are very unlikely to be able to respond as effectively. If you have strategic plans of some kind, you have a goal to pursue or a direction to take, and can focus your day-to-day management efforts on getting your unit to aim for the goal or to follow the path. Without any strategic plans you are likely to end up going nowhere in particular, and it then becomes very hard to motivate and direct your unit effectively.

So you have to plan, and because planning is itself the kind of thing that doesn't get done otherwise, you have to plan to plan. You have, in other words, to set aside regular quality time to do it. It is no good saying, as we all have a tendency to say, 'I'll plan for the future when I get around to it' or 'when I'm less busy', because you won't get around to it, you'll never be less busy, and before you know it, the future will have come and gone.

If they are to be useful, plans have to be realistic. In particular, they have to be based on realistic assumptions both as to the situations that might arise and as to your own and your unit's ability to implement what you have planned as responses to those situations – this can be a challenge. In a competitive situation, for instance, we tend to overrate our own capabilities, while underrating those of our competitors. In other contexts, too, we might be over-optimistic about some things and over-pessimistic about others. We also tend to discount possibilities that would be inconvenient or unpleasant. A striking feature of the 2008 financial crisis was that things kept happening in the markets that, according to the prevailing economists' assumptions, should only have happened once in a lifetime or once in a thousand years. They happened every week, but this never prompted the economists to question their assumptions.

The big problem with planning, of course, is that the future is always uncertain. It would be quite impossible to plan for every eventuality: the world is far too complex and far too uncertain for that. So we have to make assumptions, and even if those assumptions should accurately reflect the most probable state of future affairs, that state might still, given the vast number of possibilities, be very improbable.

Where the assumptions concerned are quantitatively expressed – an exchange rate, say, or an interest rate – we attempt to get round this by testing the sensitivity of our plans to variations in our assumptions. Will our plan still work if inflation turns out to be double what we anticipated? Where our plans rest on a single uncertain outcome, it makes sense to have alternatives. You might, for example, have two plans for how to address next year's expected challenge – one assuming that Mary chooses to come back to work after her maternity leave and one assuming that she doesn't.

In many cases, however, you will face much higher levels of uncertainty than that, with all sorts of key variables being hard to predict. To keep your plans realistic under those conditions, you will need to engage in some kind of what's sometimes called scenario planning. If you can identify several key variables – factors that would have a significant impact on your plans and are very hard to predict – and build three or four radically different scenarios, or future worlds, based on different combinations of possible outcomes, you should end up with a realistic spread of possibilities. The actual outcome may be quite different from any of the scenarios, but it's likely to lie somewhere in between them, and if you have thought through how to respond to each of the scenarios, you should have some basis for moving forward.

27 BE PREPARED FOR THE UNEXPECTED

Although you should plan, as far as possible, for what you expect to happen or, more broadly, for what you expect could happen, under different plausible scenarios, you should always be prepared for the completely unexpected. You know from experience that the unexpected happens. From natural disasters to criminal frauds, from breakthroughs to breakdowns, from personal tragedies to personal windfalls, things happen out of the blue. You can't predict them. You can't even plan for them. You have no way of knowing what might happen, and so you can't prepare for it in any specific sense. But you do know that unexpected things will happen and you can prepare yourself to deal with them when they do.

Unexpected events pose two kinds of management challenge. One is the immediate challenge of trouble-shooting: how to respond when they happen. We dealt with that earlier. The other is the challenge of how to accommodate them within a framework of planning. Scenario planning can help a lot here, as even if something isn't covered by your plausible scenarios, there's a chance that something with similar effects will be covered. The wider the range of expectations you build into your plans, the more robust they are likely to be when faced with the unexpected. More important than this, though, planning round multiple scenarios encourages you – and everyone else – to think of plans as provisional and not cast in concrete.

Just as you need to keep an open mind with respect to the interpretation of information, and to be prepared to change your mind about things when the information changes, so too with plans. Planning, even financial planning, is a kind of story-telling. It is one of the ways we reduce uncertainty, make sense of the world and get things done. Plans fix people's behaviour. They dictate that people will do certain things at certain times or in response to certain cues. But they do so on the basis of assumptions that will always be imperfect, so while their fixedness is there for a purpose, it is always somewhat artificial: a device to get things done, rather than an end in itself.

The consequence of this is that you should take plans very seriously, but never so seriously that you allow the fiction that lies behind the plan to trump the reality of events. Treat every plan as provisional and contingent upon events following roughly as expected, or within the range of the expected. Be prepared for the unexpected and be prepared to modify your plans in response.

28 DON'T BE SURPRISED WHEN YOUR PLANS ARE UPSET, BUT DO REMEMBER WHERE YOU ARE GOING

The best laid plans of mice and men will often go awry – or, in Robert Burns's original, 'The best laid schemes o' Mice an' Men, Gang aft agley, An' lea'e us nought but grief an' pain, For promis'd joy!' If your plans are based on realistic assumptions, and on a realistic view of the fragility of those assumptions, we can call them 'well laid'. But however good the planning, the implementation will always be vulnerable to unforeseen and perhaps unforeseeable accidents, sometimes of the most trivial kind. It's almost as if plans are made to be upset, and you shouldn't be at all surprised when that happens. But nor should you give up and be defeated. Keep the end in sight and work round the obstacles.

Well laid plans get upset by events, and your response to the upset should be the same as to any other event – don't panic. Think through the problem, consulting as appropriate, and act. The important thing to remember is that while your plan may have to be changed, adapted to the new circumstances, the main objectives of the plan will probably remain unchanged. Of course, this won't always be the case. A catastrophe or other major event may make the original objectives of the plan null and void. If the whole unit has to close down, for example, staff succession planning can go out of the window. If a company collapses as a result of major fraud, its strategy for growth may become an irrelevance. The more common situation, however, is more like a spanner in the works. The machinery has to be stopped, the spanner removed, any broken parts replaced and the machinery restarted, perhaps with some of the settings and procedures altered to make up for lost time, while guarding against errant spanners.

Similarly, in an organizational context, events may force you to re-jig your plans, adjust your schedules, modify your expectations and so on. But in doing all these things you should always keep in mind the aims and objectives of the plan, the direction in which you were, and probably still should be, heading. Sometimes the unexpected problems that you run into may be indicators that something has changed in the world. You may then need to change your assumptions and even modify your objectives, and/or advise your bosses of your concerns. More usually they will just be arbitrary nuisances. Satisfy yourself that this is the case, deal with the problem and then get on with executing the plan. Don't be disheartened. Don't allow yourself to get distracted. Don't give up.

29 COMMUNICATE CLEARLY AND EXPLICITLY: YOU'D BE SURPRISED HOW LITTLE PEOPLE HEAR

For a plan to be implemented effectively, it must be clearly and effectively communicated to the people doing the implementing. This applies to plans of your own making or of your own unit's making. It applies equally to plans that have been generated elsewhere in the organization, where your job may just be to plan and effect the implementation.

Communicating a strategy or plan has two main components. First, you need to communicate to people the strategy or plan itself: where the organization or unit is going and why, and how it's going to get there. Second, you need to communicate to people what's expected of them in implementing the strategy or plan and why. We shall begin with the first part.

Some managers can be quite secretive about their plans, letting people in on them only on a strictly need-to-know basis. This may be because in sharing details of a plan they feel they are giving away power in some way or because they want to avoid a public commitment to the plan, to prevent embarrassment if things go wrong. Some managers set out their plans but only vaguely, again trying to cover themselves against things going differently from what they intended. This reticence is understandable but, from an organizational perspective, it can do nothing but harm. As a basic principle, if you are trying to take an organization in any particular direction, whatever that may be and whatever kind of direction we are talking about, people need to know what the direction is.

In the best organizations, everyone knows the directions being taken, from the top management to the receptionist, to the line workers. Even if they are not actively involved in achieving the aims, their knowledge reinforces those aims and helps embed them into the culture, so that they become second nature to those who are involved in achieving them. As a manager responsible for the work of a unit, you need to tell your people where the unit and the organization as a whole are heading. And you need to tell them clearly, explicitly and repeatedly, in terms that they can understand, filling in all the gaps and not leaving them to work things out for themselves.

It is important to be explicit and to fill in the gaps because people will always tend to interpret what you say in terms of their own preconceptions. So, the more scope you leave them for interpretation, the wider of the mark they are likely to be. In thinking about the plans, whether you have drawn them up yourself or been briefed on them by your own managers, you will make all sorts of

Example 14: Thinking and Planning

We noted in the last example that Polly's administrative and troubleshooting responsibilities leave her little time for things like planning. And although the trouble-shooting eases off in the school holidays, the administration doesn't. But the sharp divide between term and holiday does help. It acts as a cue for a change of routine, and this does help her to change gear, change mindset and find some time for planning and reflection.

Rick and Brad don't have this luxury. There are always building jobs for Brad to attend to and Rick's restaurant is open fifty-two weeks a year, seven days a week. In these circumstances, planning and reflection are things they tend to do in bed or in the bath, not always when they are in the best state of mind. In an effort to cope with the stresses of work, Rick has taken to going to the gym in the mornings, and finds that a cup of coffee after working out, away from the restaurant, away from his home and (he forces himself) away from the smartphone, helps him to think more clearly about where the business is going and what he needs to be doing there.

Ed, the engineering subsidiary managing director, faces the classic challenge of senior and middle managers, which is that the higher you climb in an organization, the more time you need to spend on planning and development, but the less time you have for it, as routine administration also makes higher and higher demands. He sometimes thinks that he could manage, in the sense of keeping the company going in steady state, if he didn't also need to direct. And he could direct, in the sense of taking it forward and responding to a changing environment, if he didn't also need to manage. He really has two full-time jobs, but dividing them up wouldn't work either because anyone trying to direct the company without the day-to-day experience of managing it, just wouldn't understand the challenges.

Ed's approach is to look at this as if it were an engineering problem. Engineers don't usually seek 'perfect' solutions. They seek solutions that are good enough to get the job done, with compromises if necessary, and with sufficient tolerances to protect against failure. So every Sunday night Ed reviews his commitments and deadlines for the week ahead, works out what compromises need to be made to make it all do-able, and adjusts his plans accordingly. He also makes sure his diary is free for the early part of one morning, and that morning he goes in even earlier than usual and gives himself some planning time. (Ed doesn't like taking work home, so that Sunday review is the only work he does do from home – for him taking work home would just make things even more stressful and probably less productive.)

The other thing Ed does is to arrange, every three months, for one of the youngsters in the firm to be seconded to his office for a week. He knows he's not the most creative thinker himself, so he lays out some of his current problems, leaves the youngsters to explore them and at the end of the week argues things out with them. It's good learning for them, he reasons, and good input for him. It gets him into thinking mode and opens his mind to thoughts he wouldn't have himself.

For the perils of plans going astray, we can go back to Rick and the restaurant. Leasing the building, designing and fitting the interiors, equipping the kitchen, recruiting staff and marketing the new venue was a major project, and while everything was carefully planned out, nothing worked out according to plan. It's not that the plans had been unrealistic. The owner's initial business plan, it is true, was totally unrealistic. He'd wanted to leverage his own investment with bank loans and the lending bank – Belle's bank, as it happens – had cut his proposition down to size. They had also introduced Rick to a small-business consultant who had helped him work out sensible budgets and lead times, and put together a marketing strategy. Still, it seemed, everything that could go wrong did go wrong. Planning permission for the facade was refused. The building work was delayed. The kitchen suppliers went bust, and when a kitchen was installed, the chef they had appointed said he didn't like it and took a job in Barcelona. The opening was delayed three times, and a prominent restaurant critic then came on the worst night possible, with the chef in bed with the 'flu.

Rick persevered, and the owner (eventually) stumped up to meet the extra costs, but it required great resourcefulness and tremendous patience.

assumptions that have become embedded in your mind, through the planning process or through discussions at the managerial level. But they might not be embedded in the minds of the people who work for you. Indeed, it is quite likely that their assumptions, developed in a pre-plan context, are completely different. So you always need to think about what they will hear when your words are translated into their mindsets and not what you hear when you speak those words to yourself. If you're in any doubt at all, spell things out, in words of one syllable. Ask them to feed back to you what they have heard and explicitly address not only any misconceptions you detect, but also any fuzziness.

The 'repeatedly' bit is also important. One of the classic rules of leadership is 'communicate, communicate, communicate'. Don't just say things once, because people don't always listen, and even when they do listen – even when they can feed back to you accurately what you've said – they don't always retain what they've heard and don't always register its importance. So say what you have to say again and again, over a period of time. And keep saying it, as you go through the implementation. Keep refreshing people's minds and keep the message in focus. It is very easy to assume that when people have 'got it', they will hold on to it. In practice, however, they are very likely to lose it, or at least drift off it. What was clear at the beginning becomes vague or distorted as time goes on. Old habits and old assumptions reassert themselves, and new distractions get in the way. It's a bit like walking in the open countryside. You can set off with a very clear idea of where you are going and the path you will be following, but unless you check your map from time to time, you can very easily drift off the path and get completely lost.

You may feel that all this explicit detail and constant repetition shouldn't be necessary, but it almost always is. You may fear that people will find you a pain or a bore, but they won't. If you repeat yourself too much in one session, yes – there is nothing more tedious than when, in a meeting, people just keep repeating themselves. In that context, once or maybe twice for emphasis is probably enough. But the point here is to have a series of meetings and keep putting across the same consistent message each time.

30 EXPLAIN WHERE YOU ARE GOING – USE STORIES, MAPS AND PICTURES

If you're trying to communicate something new or something complex, clarity, explicitness and repetition are all important, but they're often not enough. Communications will only be effective if they are meaningful. Words acquire meaning from their context, so what a sentence means to you will depend on what you bring to it, consciously or unconsciously, from other things in your mind: your assumptions and ways of thinking about people and places, about the organization, about its context, about human nature and so on. These will depend on your particular attitudes, your particular beliefs and your particular unique set of experiences. The same is true for anyone else, only their attitudes, beliefs and experiences will be different, perhaps very different, from yours. So what is in their mind will also be very different from what is in yours. Being very explicit and very specific will help you to break through this contextual framing, to challenge the meaning people would naturally give to your words. But to really communicate effectively you need to go a step further and provide them with new meanings, with a new meaningful context that can replace the old one.

We typically find meaning in stories of one kind or another: in novels, plays, histories, poems and movies, but also in music and dance, in paintings and sculptures, and, at a simple level, in maps. What all these different modes of story-telling have in common is that they connect things – words, images, ideas – in rich webs of meaning. So a sentence spoken by a character in a play or a movie means little in isolation, but a lot in the context of the work as a whole. Even a statement of historical fact may have all sorts of different meanings, depending on how it is contextualized by the historian. And even an ordinary map, through a selection of what is shown and what is not shown, encourages you to make certain connections between places or objects and so to make sense of those, to give them meaning, in a particular way.

Of course the meaning attributed to something by a reader or listener is never in the control of the writer or speaker. People will always add their own interpretive layers on to the story and replace your intended meanings with their own. But the richer and more persuasive the story you tell, the more likely you are to get your meaning across. So draw people maps. Use pictures, charts and diagrams, and take care what you use – not just whatever you can find. Many Powerpoint demonstrations, highly illustrated as they may be, are mind-numbing, totally devoid of meaning. Above all, make use of words. Tell a story about the direction you are going and why that is both absorbing and convincing. We say that a good story captures people's imaginations and that is precisely what you are after, because it is in the imagination, above all, that meaning lurks.

You have to be careful that in telling your story you don't distort your message, by letting your own imagination run away with you. Some teachers keep their classes enthralled but don't actually teach them what they intend to. The requirement for accuracy, clarity and explicitness always comes first. But if you can combine this with a story that captures people's imaginations, then you have the basis for effective communication.

31 MAKE SURE PEOPLE KNOW WHAT IS EXPECTED OF THEM – AND WHY

The second part of effective communication is about communicating to people what's expected of them: what you need them to do and why. The 'what' bit of this is straightforward. You can't expect people to do what you want if you don't tell them what you want. And, as with any other communication, you need to be explicit, to make yourself clear and to provide an appropriate level of detail. Some people will catch on easily to what you expect of them, but others will need it spelling out, task by task and point by point. This will become much easier if you can also get the 'why' bit right.

Explaining why you expect things of people is all about tying the task into the story you're telling about where the unit or the organization is going. If you've told the story well and engaged people in it, they will want to know what parts they have to play. If the story is welcome, if it holds out lots of promise, they will want to play a part and be keen to know what that part is. But even if the story is unwelcome – if they feel threatened by it, for example, as they might with a story of retrenchment or consolidation – they will want to know how it affects them. They will want to know what parts they are expected to play, even if they don't really want to play them.

If you have told the story really well, some people will recognize their parts without any further explanation. But others won't, and still others will jump to the wrong conclusions or cast themselves in totally inappropriate roles. So even if you have set out a first-rate drama, you will still need to be a hands-on director and spell out all the different parts and who is to play them.

If people not only know what they are expected to do but also have a meaningful sense of why they are expected to do it, how it fits in to the overall plan, they are much more likely to do it well. The strong context will keep the task in focus and reduce the risk of backsliding. The understanding of why they are doing it will also help them to respond appropriately and to adapt to any problems they meet along the way. Suppose, for example, that something extraneous interferes with a task they have to do. The more they know about why they are doing it, the better placed they will be to respond in the way you would hope, and the better motivated they will be to look for such a response.

Even if people are assigned unwelcome tasks, perhaps as a result of unwelcome strategies, having the full reasons behind those tasks will make it harder for them to thwart the implementation by intentional, or more likely semi-intentional, non-performance. If people know what's expected of them but have nothing of the background as to why, it becomes easy to fudge things and not quite do what is wanted. If they have the background, if they have a clear reason for the task, such fudging becomes much harder. Non-performance becomes more explicit and is more easily challenged.

32 ACT AS YOU WOULD ASK OTHERS TO ACT – YOU WOULD BE SURPRISED HOW MUCH PEOPLE NOTICE

If one of the truths of communication is that people don't always listen when you want them to and don't always hear what you say when they do listen, another is that they often watch when you don't want them to and are quick to notice what they see. In particular, if any of your actions are at odds with your words, or at odds with the actions you are asking of them, they will notice. At least, someone will notice, the word will get quickly around, your credibility will be damaged and it will be that much harder to get people either to hear what you say or to do as you ask.

This is most obvious in the case of ethics. If you tell people to be kind and are observed being cruel, or if you tell people to be altruistic and are observed being selfish, you will just be branded a hypocrite and any moral instruction you give will, quite probably, be ignored. The same principle applies, however, across a wide range of behaviour. You cannot ask people to be punctual and expect them to be so, if you are not punctual yourself. They might obey, out of fear of reprimand or out of their own sense of duty, but even if they do, they will feel aggrieved. Your reputation will suffer and they will look for opportunities to get their own back. In much the same way, you can't expect people to follow any policy you set out, or at least to follow it happily, if you exempt yourself, whether explicitly or by default. And you can't expect people to play their parts in pursuing a strategy or plan if your actions and decisions suggest any lack of commitment on your own part.

Managers are not as exposed to this kind of risk as are some other groups, like politicians, for example. A key feature of the work of politicians is that they have to make all sorts of public commitments: to political principles, policies, priorities and plans. To get elected, moreover, they have to make such commitments on all sorts of issues and to appeal in the process to all sorts of voters' hopes and fears, preferences and prejudices. Another key feature is that they come, like celebrities, under intense public scrutiny in every-

---

Example 15: Communication, Communication, Communication

While the basic rules of communication apply everywhere, the particular challenges vary from one context to another. Both Melanie and Belle have to implement policies decided elsewhere – in the Foundation Trust, in Melanie's case, and the bank head-quarters, in Belle's – and to communicate these to their staff. But the different contexts raise different issues.

In a large hospital, word gets round incredibly quickly, and this makes Melanie's task both easier and harder. It's easier because if there is a new policy, everybody will be talking about it and everybody will know about it. She doesn't have to impress on people that things are changing. It's harder because the informal communications are out of anybody's control. People develop their own versions of what the policy means and of its relevance or otherwise to their jobs. Melanie not only has to tell a story, but also has to impose that particular story over the many other stories circulating. This requires clarity, precision and constant illustration through examples: in this situation, we do this. Why? Because. She is used to this, because even when there is nothing new to be communicated, she is always having to manage agency nurses, who arrive with experiences of differ-ent hospitals and different ways of doing things, and have to be inducted into the practices of her wards. But she is constantly surprised by how much she needs to do to communicate with her core team.

In contrast to the constant interactions of the hospital, Belle's local high street bank branch is in something of a bubble, largely isolated from the rest of the organization. Staff come and go, and they interact with their peers elsewhere on training courses, but what they know of the bank is essentially down to their experi-ence of the branch, and to a certain extent that's true for her too. So she doesn't have to cope with such a wide variety of differ-

thing that they do. Hypocrisy is unavoidable. Managers work in a more private sphere. Unless they are the chief executives of major listed corporations, their plans and policies, and the instructions that go with them, are typically aired only within the organization, and they are able to keep their home lives both private and quite

ent stories, but she does have to work much harder to make her own story meaningful – to make connections between the rather remote strategies of the bank and the immediate demands of their implementation. She finds that to get things across she needs to schedule workshops and discussion sessions, and that even when she's got a story across, she needs constant repetition to make it stick.

The relative isolation of a local branch is also an issue for George, as, although he moves quite a lot between the branches of the car dealership, the people who work under him don't. And whereas the bank's staff have uniforms, are surrounded by corporate marketing materials and even see their bank's strategies communicated through television and newspaper advertisements, so they are in no doubt that they are part of a much bigger organization, that doesn't apply in the garage. Communicating branch-level policies is relatively straightforward, but the whole idea of a corporate policy is hard to get across.

With his own small building business, Brad's communications task is in many ways much simpler than those facing managers in larger organizations. He has the authority to hold his audience and he has a story that is his story, so it can be put across forcefully with no danger of it appearing remote and irrelevant, and no danger of confusion from rival versions. But he is under no illusions that he can just say something and expect people to act. His employees are not generally good listeners, and he has to hammer home his messages, again and again.

Brad has also found that he is extraordinarily exposed. He tries to reinforce his messages by walking the walk, as well as talking the talk. He wants his staff to treat clients in a certain way, for example, so he makes sure that they see him treating them that way. But he can act out his messages day after day with no-one seeming to take a blind bit of notice – then one slight slip when he's stressed and tired, and everybody's on to it, as an excuse to let their own behaviour slide.

separate from their work. Within their organizations, however, and especially within their units, they are closely watched. People will always look to their managers' actions for cues as to how to behave and what to say themselves. So, to preserve your effectiveness as a manager, you have to make sure that your actions conform to your words.

33 BE YOURSELF

Keeping your words and actions in line with each other is much easier if you don't have to put on an act – if you mean what you say and do as you mean; if you are yourself and true to yourself. You can't always be completely yourself at work. At least, you can't always be completely what you think of as yourself, or what your most intimate friends or family would recognize as yourself. But you can normally be true to yourself in the things that matter most, and the more of that true self you can bring to work, the better.

Work will always be an artificial situation. You are paid, after all, to do what suits the organization or its owners, rather than what you might otherwise choose to do. In accepting a contract for employment you inevitably give up some freedom of choice, not only in terms of how you spend your time but also in terms of how you act. So the 'person' who appears at work is never quite the same as the 'person' who appears at home, and at times might be very different, for very good reasons. Your intimates, for example, will tolerate personality traits, behaviours, moods or quirks that would be quite out of place at work: being grumpy in the mornings, perhaps, or quick-tempered when people irritate you, or argumentative, or having pet hates or prejudices. As a manager you will need to overcome these or set them aside, and while the result may not be the true you, it will probably be a slightly better you.

More significantly, you may find yourself working in an organization or line of business with which you are not really sympathetic. This happens all the time: we all need to earn a living and we can't always get the ideal job. So we have to take what we can get and make the most of it. Or you may find yourself out of sympathy, personally, with the strategy that the organization is pursuing. If you are a civil servant, say, or working in health, social services or education, you may have to implement a government policy with which you strongly disagree. Even in a business setting, you may feel that the strategy or plan to which the company has committed is misconceived and, if you are someone who relishes the challenges of business, you might feel quite strongly about that. The true 'you' might want to contest the strategy and keep contesting it, while the employed 'you' is charged with accepting and implementing it.

In cases like these, you will clearly have to suppress an important part of yourself, but you will do so by drawing on other important parts of yourself: a commitment to professionalism and the democratic process, if you are a civil servant; a commitment to contractual and agent obligations, if you are in business. And you will set this in the context of something even more important. An employer buys your time, your commitment and certain aspects of your behaviour: an element of mechanistic loyalty (or at least non-disloyalty), for example, and of obedience within reason. An employer does not, however, buy you outright, and there are certain core aspects of yourself that are implicitly untouched by the employment contract. Most basically, these include your human rights, but they also include more than that: the values and sympathies that enable you as a person to interact with other people, including the integrity and humanity we discussed earlier.

Focused as they are on outputs and performance, and the quantitative measures that go with these, neither businesses nor public sector bureaucracies have much time for non-monetary values (or values that can't be translated into monetary terms), whether of the ethical or any other kind. This is partly a consequence of size and the anonymity that goes with that; partly of bureaucratization, which replaces personal judgements with impersonal rules; and partly of business school teaching, which has always stressed the technical aspects of management, as against the personal. Things like personal loyalty, friendship, collegiality, sympathy, kindness and so on are treated as being outside work and as having, essentially, no part in work. It's not that employers deny your right to have values, but the systems encourage you to take them home with you and not let them interfere with the work of the organization.

The trouble is, these values are precisely what make organizations work effectively, and make people work effectively within them! They are priceless, not only in the sense that you can't put a price or profit figure on them, but also in the sense that they are beyond pricing. Without them, pricing itself would be irrelevant.

Effective managers don't leave their values at home. They control their emotions: they don't let love affairs interfere with work, for example. But they do bring to work all the values and value-based behaviours that make them human and help them to interact positively with other humans. As far as they can, and within the limits imposed by the situations they find themselves in, they bring their whole living selves to work, and not just some mechanical replicas.

34 HOLD ON TO YOUR MORALS – STAY MORALLY ENGAGED

Some of the most important values that any of us hold are our basic ethical or moral values. These vary somewhat from one person to another. One person thinks in terms of duties and obligations, another in terms of equality or fairness. One person draws specifically from Christian moral teaching, another from Islam and another from Harry Potter. When it comes to things like cheating, lying or pilfering, few of us are paragons of virtue, and we all draw the lines between what is and what is not morally acceptable slightly differently. On life and death matters, like abortion or euthanasia or the morality of war, and on matter of sex and sexuality, we might hold quite contrasting views. But on most everyday matters, and certainly on most of those likely to arise in the context of work, there is a remarkable level of agreement. We all know, roughly speaking, what is right and wrong. And yet business and other organizations repeatedly get into ethical difficulties.

The problem is not that organizations set out collectively to do wrong. There is a widespread consensus, across sectors and across countries, that business and organizational activities should be conducted morally. (The only exception is the financial sector of business where, for reasons largely to do with the demoralizing effects of money and the influence of economic theory, moral considerations don't seem to apply.) It is also well understood that while unethical behaviours may be profitable in the short term – in a competitive situation, being unconstrained by morals gives you a competitive edge – they are almost always disastrous in the longer term. So, organizations very rarely set out to be unethical.

But individuals within organizations, or in control of organizations, do sometimes act unethically, for their private gain, and what is remarkable is how blind the people in and around these organizations can be to what is going on. There will always be a few people who are immoral, but their immorality only gets out of control and causes serious harm to large numbers of people when they are allowed to get away with it over an extended period. In ordinary life, people are morally aware, they notice when someone is behaving badly. In organizations, the pressures of work, the pressure for performance and the general tendency to exclude or discount questions of value, all contribute to people not noticing and not being morally aware. Look at any of the big ethical scandals of recent decades and you will see that in each case numbers of people, in some cases extremely large numbers of people, were in a position to see what was going on, but somehow managed not to.

The people in a position to notice any unethical behaviours in an organization are its managers. They are the people who are tapped into the information networks. As a manager, moral awareness will not be part of your formal job description, and the practices of the organization may make it hard for you to achieve. But it is implicitly part of the job, and a very important part too. Unless they are corrupt themselves, your bosses will want you not to leave your morals at home, but to bring them with you to work. And they will want you to be morally aware and engaged. The question is, how do you do this, given all the obstacles in your way?

The challenge you face is similar to the one you face in planning. Moral awareness requires observation and reflection, and in a typical work situation you will have neither the time to observe and reflect nor the state of mind you would need for that. Time for managers is always at a premium – there is always too much to do and the pressure for performance makes it very hard to concentrate on anything else. Strategy and planning are at least directly related to performance. The shift from routine administration and coping with events to planning is a shift of mindset, but it's not as big a shift as that to questions of ethics and morals.

The challenge is made greater because while strategy and planning can be concentrated into discrete periods of time, moral awareness needs to be ongoing. Fortunately it is also made possible because, if you don't actively shut out your emotional sensitivity, it will continue to act unconsciously. When something is going wrong around us, even if we don't notice it consciously, we feel a sense of unease. And when someone around us is uneasy, we pick that up too, even if we don't consciously notice the cause.

So what you need to bring to the problem are: first, an attitude of emotional engagement that will allow any feelings of unease to penetrate your consciousness; and, second, some regular time for reflection on your feelings. The first part is just about being yourself and not erecting barriers to your normal emotional responses. The second part requires very little time – just long enough, most of the time, to satisfy yourself that your emotional responses are still working, and to open your mind to any sense of unease; and a little longer, very occasionally, to analyse the sources of that unease.

Example 16: Being Yourself

For most of our managers, 'being themselves' wasn't much of a problem. They either worked for themselves or in organizations where people were expected to be... well, people. Several had experiences of other kinds, however.

George's experiences came out when he was having a drink one evening with a former colleague, Harry, now working for a different firm. They'd been discussing the movie *The Wolf of Wall Street* and the endless stories about unethical behaviour in the investment banks, from money-laundering to harassment and from fiddling rates to mis-selling financial products. How, said Harry, could people behave like that, and how could nobody notice what was going on? Well, said George, when he was a young man he had worked for a large second-hand car dealer in Birmingham. It wasn't the sort of place you wouldn't buy a second-hand car from. They didn't sell cars that were unsafe or hide their defects. They could just as easily have been selling agricultural equipment, or anything else for that matter. But they were fixated on turning a profit. Everybody was on commission and there was an aggressively competitive and very male culture. They would all try to out-do each other, not only by getting high prices for poor products, but also in the stories they told and their general behaviour. It wasn't, he suspected, unlike an invest-ment bank, except that the amounts of money were much, much smaller.

In this context, he said, two things happened. One was that his social behaviour began to mirror his work behaviour. He didn't have a stable family background, he wanted to be accepted and he went along with what was on offer. The other was that, as he discovered later, the firm became used as a vehicle for money-laundering by the local drugs' baron. Cars were coming and going at silly prices, that made no commercial sense, so it should have been obvious, but since silly prices were what the salesmen were about, they just hooted and saw them as great deals.

By the time the firm was closed down, George had a cocaine habit, had narrowly escaped a conviction for date rape and had landed someone with a six-month-old child he had no intention at the time of supporting. Somehow he got through, got a job at a respectable dealership and worked his way up – not by 'being himself', because the self he started out with was a complete mess, but by being the self he should have been. In his case, the work George had been different from the home George but better – and gradually the home George had followed. The responsibilities of management had prepared him for the responsibilities of family.

Before he had become a restaurant manager, Rick had worked in the kitchens, first of pubs and then of restaurants. Here too the culture had been aggressively masculine, often violent and quite unlike anything he had experienced before. His family had hardly been functional, but he had a typical middle-class upbringing, had been to university and thought he knew good from bad. Rick's solution to the problem posed had been to create a mask but to use that mask to protect his true self. So, pressed for lewd stories about his background and off-site behaviour, he made them up, and he cursed and swore like everyone else, but he was never taken in by his own act, and when things got beyond what he could accept, he just moved on. Then, when he got into management roles, he gradually began to ditch the act and bring his own values to the organizations in which he worked.

The other manager to have experienced unethical behaviour was Belle, whose bank had been fined large amounts for mis-selling financial insurance products that were quite inappropriate for the customers' needs. Belle hadn't been involved in any of the mis-selling herself and hadn't really registered that anything was wrong. She assumed that the bank had properly researched the products and that the product description and the instructions given to the sales' staff were fine. She knew that the staff themselves had no conception whatsoever that they might be doing anything wrong. There was something about the approach – a hard sell of products that didn't really seem to add up – that made her uneasy, and she had some questions, but she assumed that those questions had been asked and answered higher up the managerial chain, so she didn't say anything. And, indeed, if she had said anything it probably wouldn't have made any difference. But, she thought afterwards, if lots of branch managers had said something, or if any of the regional managers had said anything...

35 BE HONEST WITH YOURSELF AND OTHERS

One of the most fundamental ethical values, and one that is expected of any manager, is truthfulness or honesty. As we've already noted, however, people have different views as to what honesty entails. For some people it requires telling the literal truth, the whole truth and nothing but the truth, but most of us are much less demanding, both of ourselves and of others. In fact we tell little fibs and hide bits of the truth all the time, whether to avoid hurting people, to avoid complications and make life easier for ourselves, to present ourselves in a better light, out of laziness or even to have fun, if we think it will do no great harm. We all accept that there are limits, however, even if we define them differently, and that there is a difference between being fundamentally honest (if never completely honest) and being seriously dishonest.

In practice, we can probably draw two lines, both of which are important in managing. One is an ethical line and is about being honest with other people. The other is harder to classify but is about being honest with ourselves.

If you hope to be trusted as a manager, you have to be honest with people, and what this means in practice is not misleading them. We have discussed the importance of giving people information about the direction you are going and the context that makes sense of this, but you always have to be careful what you say and the requirement of honesty will often be a limiting factor. There will always be things you can't say, because to do so would betray a personal or organizational confidence, or would imply an opinion or judgement that is not appropriately shared (say, a judgement on someone's performance) and would itself be a breach of trust. People generally understand this. There will also be things you can't talk about because what you could say, being incomplete, would be open to misinterpretation. If there is a chance that people might get the wrong end of the stick, you can be sure someone will take it.

So you have to choose your words very carefully and to tell a truth that is not the whole truth but is, so to speak, in the spirit of the truth: no outright falsehood, no attempt to deceive, but rather an attempt to be as open and honest as you can – in the circumstances. Sometimes the circumstances will demand reticence, and sometimes you will need to explain this reticence, reminding people that you have a duty of confidence to others, as well as to them, or explaining that in a fluid and complex situation any attempt at an accurate summary would be likely to mislead. Whatever you choose to say, however, your choice should be guided by a simple rule: if someone else was in your position and made this same choice, and you knew about it, would it compromise your trust in their honesty and integrity?

There may of course be situations, especially in a business context or perhaps a diplomatic one, where you have to mislead people for a time. A worthwhile objective might only be achievable by preserving a fiction, and the fiction itself might do no lasting harm. So you are called on to be temporarily dishonest, trusted to be temporarily untrustworthy. OK, but only so long as it is temporary, that you are able to explain it in retrospect and that it passes the test just mentioned.

The test itself is not straightforward, however, as it requires you to be honest with yourself and this can also be very challenging. It can be quite hard to take an honest, objective view of yourself. In a strict sense it's impossible. The image you have of yourself is the product of the stories you tell yourself about yourself. These in turn are influenced by the stories you tell about yourself to other people, and by the stories they tell you about yourself. All these stories are, like all stories, selective. They emphasize some things, de-emphasize others and leave many things out completely. We all typically gloss over our little faults and suppress our big ones, creating images with which we can live comfortably.

We can't be completely and utterly honest with ourselves – it's impossible. But we can fall back on the same criterion we use when judging honesty to others. Being honest with yourself, in practical terms, means simply not fooling yourself, not kidding yourself that you are better (or indeed worse) than you are or that you are fundamentally different from what you are.

It also means not kidding yourself that circumstances or events or people are fundamentally different from what they are. If you see the world through rose-coloured spectacles, you will not only fool yourself, you will also mislead anyone who depends on your judgement. Similarly, if you see everyone as devious and manipulative, or as paragons of virtue, or if you allow your judgement to be clouded by your hopes or fears, loves or hates. You can only avoid misleading other people if you first avoid misleading yourself.

Like planning or moral awareness, this requires reflection, and in this case critical self-reflection. It is not just about work, like planning is, or about overcoming the obstacles of work, as in maintaining moral awareness. It is fundamentally about how you live your life, and build and develop your character. But our working selves and our home selves are never quite the same, and the working self is probably more prone to self-deception. The context is narrower and more artificial, and the stories we tell ourselves about ourselves are also narrower and more artificial. So, in reflecting on how honest you are with yourself, you do need to pay special attention to your working self and to do this you need, ironically, to get as far away from work as you can, so as to get the critical objectivity you need. This is definitely one for the holidays.

36 SEEK HELP WHEN YOU NEED IT

One of the ways in which we consistently fool ourselves is in thinking that we can manage without help from others. We fool ourselves into thinking that we can cope when we can't, that we are in control when we are barely coping or that we've reached the best solution to a problem when we've only reached part of a solution. Part of this is prompted by embarrassment or pride: we don't want to admit to our failures or weaknesses. Part of it is wishful thinking: we turn our hopes into beliefs. Part of it is to do with preserving a false self-image: we don't want to admit our limitations, even to ourselves.

The ridiculous thing about this is that we would all agree that other people should seek help when they need it – it is only for ourselves that we make an exception. But whereas making an exception for ourselves usually acts at least in our short-term self-interest, this particular exception is in no-one's best interest. If you try to cope when you can't, or kid yourself that you're in control when you're not, or kid yourself that you've reached the best solution or chosen the best path when you haven't, you don't gain anything, even in the short term. And other people lose.

Two practical questions arise. One is about timing: how can you identify the point at which you need help? The other is about direction: where should you go to for help? In fact they are related, because if you have people you can call on for help, and they are the right people for the purpose, they will also be able to detect – quite probably before you do – when you need help. In a domestic situation, you will look to your close friends or your loved ones; or rather, they will look out for you. They will see if you are stressed or struggling or out of your depth. They will sense if you are not really achieving as much as you claim or as much as you could, and they will usually be willing to help if only you will let them. They may offer advice on the matter in question or they may suggest you see someone else – a doctor, perhaps, or a lawyer or even just a family friend. Or they may just offer essential emotional support while you work through something for yourself.

In a work context, the people you will naturally look to are your own manager, or perhaps one of your more experienced managerial colleagues. You can't choose your manager or your colleagues in the way that you choose your friends, and they are not going to know you anything like as well as your friends and family know you. But if they are doing their jobs well, they should still be able to help. They will generally have experience of the kinds of problems you face, they will understand the context and they will be able to look at your problems more objectively than you can. They may also provide links to other resources in the organization – pools of knowledge and experience of which you may be unaware, or which you may have forgotten about. And, if nothing else, they will be able to provide a sounding board. When a problem becomes difficult and we begin to get stressed about it, when we need to take a broader view, this is precisely when we tend to take a narrower, more blinkered view. And the best way to counter this is by sharing your thoughts with other people. They may not even have to say anything. Sometimes in talking to them you will automatically anticipate their responses and see what's gone missing from your own perspective.

Quite often work problems and more personal problems interact. So, stresses at home may limit your capacity to keep on top of things at work, or stresses caused by work may rebound on your family or threaten your own health and well-being. This is, of course, a problem, but it also presents an opportunity, and the solution is emphatically not to separate the two worlds. If you are struggling at work, it is quite likely that someone close to you outside of work – your partner or a very close friend – will be the first to notice. Similarly, if you are struggling at home, it may well be your colleagues at work who notice it first. Precisely because they are not involved in the problem, they pick up the small changes of behaviour that are signs of stress, which is a good indication of when you need help. You need help with a work problem when your loved ones notice that you have a problem, and you need help with a home problem when your closest work colleagues notice that you have a problem. All this assumes, of course, that you do talk a bit about your work to your loved ones, and that you are open in a personal sense with your work colleagues. Often what they will notice is precisely that you stop talking and go silent. But that is just about being an ordinary, integral, human being.

37 BE QUIETLY ASSERTIVE, NOT AGGRESSIVE OR DEFENSIVE

Whether you are on top of things or not, one of the inevitable consequences of management responsibility is criticism. You will be called on to make judgements and, having made them, you will be challenged and criticized. Sometimes the criticism can be very aggressive, not necessarily because of anything you have done, but because some people are just like that. How you respond is important.

Example 17: Being Honest With Yourself

Most of our managers had to manage one or two people who found it difficult to be honest with themselves, to seek help or to heed advice. Some lacked confidence in their abilities and blamed themselves whenever anything went wrong. Others thought they knew it all and could do it all. They wouldn't ask anyone for help, wouldn't listen to good advice and would never accept that they'd made a mistake. Managing people like this, building them up and setting them free from their doubts or bringing them to understand their limitations, is something that all managers have to do at one time or another. But few managers are immune from the same problems themselves.

In George's case, for example, the mess he got into as a young man, described in the last example, was closely linked to these kinds of issues: a lack of self-confidence and a tendency to cover this up rather than seek the help he needed to overcome it. But in the long run that experience has served him well. He has a good sense of what he can do and what he can't, of when he should be giving help and when he should be seeking it.

Brad's weakness is that he always thinks he can do much more than he really can. He has a tendency to take on too much and is reluctant to admit when he's over-stretched or out of his depth. The safety valve here is home. His wife can sense when he's not being quite honest with himself and she can talk to him about it in a way in which no-one at work ever could.

Ed and Belle are perhaps the luckiest of our managers in this context. Both have reached management positions through standard career paths in large organizations, and both have been helped a lot by their own managers. Belle, though she manages her own staff very well, still doubts her own judgement and still hasn't fulfilled her potential as a result. But her regular appraisals in the bank have brought this out, help is at hand and she's learnt enough to be able to accept it. Ed, on the other hand, has reached his level. He is very good at his job and has thought that

Quite often the strongest challenges come from the people least qualified to make them. They may be experts at managing in their own particular context and judge your actions on the grounds appropriate to that context, and not to yours. They think they are being helpful and constructive, but what you experience is criticism

---

he would be capable of more, that he could one day be the group chief executive. But he would not be anything like so good if he were promoted. The good thing is that he knows this, in his heart of hearts, and his bosses know it too.

Polly, the primary school head, is at a much earlier stage of her career and is still learning about herself. We've already come across part of this learning in earlier examples. She has learnt, for example, to curtail a tendency to make prompt judgements and to hold back from saying or doing things until she is sure of her ground. She also learnt one valuable lesson quite early on in her headship when she had come under a strong attack from one of the governors at a governing body meeting. The gist of the attack was that her measured approach – letting things settle down after a difficult period and learning about the school and its problems before trying to solve them – was wrong and a sign of incompetence. That wasn't quite what the governor said, but it was clearly what she thought. That put Polly on the defensive, and as the attack hardened and another of the governors seemed to join in, she became quite aggressive, in a quiet, tight-lipped way, herself. Neither of these governors had run schools them-selves. One, a parent governor, was a head-hunter, the other retired from the army.

After the meeting another of the governors took her aside and arranged another meeting. At this meeting he explained, in a supportive way, that while she was probably right, she had made life much more difficult for herself. The head-hunter was now convinced that she was a complete wally and quite incompetent. And the colonel, who had a lot more relevant experience than she realized, had actually been trying to help her.

Polly still tenses up when the head-hunter speaks and she hasn't got rid of her defensiveness, but she did come back at the next meeting with some constructive responses. She did take on board what the colonel had suggested and she's gradually getting better at building on criticism, rather than just reacting to it.

that is unhelpful and destructive. It is very easy to get annoyed by such situations and all too easy to get defensive. You insist that the issue has been properly researched and the right people consulted, and you firmly restate your position. You strongly imply that, with the greatest respect, your critics don't know what they're talking about, but you do. And if their questioning has been aggressive, you respond aggressively: you give as good as you get.

Sometimes your critics will be uninformed and your judgement will be impeccable. But even then a defensive or defensive-aggressive response will be counter-productive. You may see yourself as being firm, but your critics will see you as being obstinate and as refusing to listen to criticism or advice. When next an issue arises, they will start out from this assumption and almost inevitably quarrel with you again, raising the stakes – and raising your hackles – still further. Nothing good can come of this.

Sometimes your critics may have a point, even if it's not the point they think they have. Your judgements will never be perfect, after all, however much work and consultation has gone into them. In such cases what gets lost is the issue in question. A defensive response closes off discussion and puts you into a corner. The more strongly you stand by your position, the more committed you will be to it and the harder you will find it to reassess it in the future.

The best response to criticism is not to block it off but to encourage it. If someone makes a challenge you consider wrong or misguided, ask them to expand on their reasoning. Present yourself as keen to learn from them and be genuinely keen to learn from them, albeit that what you learn may not always be what they intended to teach. And don't give an instant judgement on their judgement. Thank them for their input and say that you will take it away and think about it, and, by the way, can you come back to them for more help when you're ready. Assert yourself, but assert your responsible self – not a self that knows best, because you know you don't always know best; not even a self that is trying its best, because while you probably are trying your best that is not what is at issue. It would be at issue if your manager criticized you for not trying, but when someone is criticizing your judgement, it is your judgement that is in question, not your effort. Assert the self that wants to reach the best judgement, is open to critical inputs and is willing to revise judgements in the light of such inputs.

Above all, don't meet aggression with aggression – or with mocking satire, contempt or anything else that risks raising the temperature. Duels are not productive. Just behave, or try to behave, as if your challenger was not aggressive at all: or as if the aggression was like a speech defect or disability of some kind, requiring a greater effort on your part but not prejudicing your view of the person or the person's capabilities.

38 DEVOLVE RESPONSIBILITY AS MUCH AS YOU CAN – NEVER DEVOLVE BLAME

While managing your critical peers can be a trial, the most important part of any manager's job is managing your own staff. We have already discussed some of the basic principles involved: humanity and integrity, trust and respect, admitting to, and forgiving, mistakes. We now turn to some more specific guidelines, beginning with the question of how much responsibility you should devolve.

The simple rule is that you should devolve as much responsibility as you can or, in other words, as much as people can manage. This will often be significantly more than you think they can manage, for obvious reasons. You will be more conscious of their weaknesses, since these are what you have to deal with on a day-to-day basis, than of their strengths. You will want to keep control. You won't want to risk the performance of your unit. You won't want to risk your own reputation. For all these reasons your instincts will be to be cautious, just as a parent's instincts are to be cautious over the freedom they give to a teenager. But you will almost certainly be over-cautious.

One of the lessons we learn from bringing up children is that, providing you are prepared to trust them, they will generally repay that trust, far more than you might think. The situation with adults at work is much the same. There are clearly cases where you can't safely devolve responsibility, because people don't have the competence, the confidence or the expertise to do what is needed. But where nothing fundamental is lacking, people will generally rise to the challenge. Just because they haven't shown particular talents, doesn't mean that they don't have them: they might just not have had the chance to show them or, if they've had the chance, then not the incentive.

Of course, devolving responsibility is not the same as giving up responsibility. The fact that you make someone responsible for a task doesn't in any way absolve you of responsibility for it. You will have to mentor them. You will have at first to monitor them, though this will have to be unobtrusive if it is not to be disabling. You will have to be prepared to take the responsibility away again, if things work out badly. But you should never do this too quickly.

You must give people time to learn and, if necessary, to learn from their mistakes.

Devolving responsibility is also not the same as devolving accountability. If you choose to delegate responsibility for something to one of your team, you remain accountable for that decision and for its consequences. If things go wrong, it is you who will be answerable and you who will have to take the blame, if there is any. You cannot, as a manager, give someone responsibility for something and then blame them if, for whatever reason, they are not up to exercising it. To do so would be to treat them unfairly, and all it would achieve, apart from the hurt, would be damage to your own reputation. Even if the person you trusted is clearly at fault, it is still your fault that you trusted them, and blaming them for what has gone wrong will just come across as an attempt to exonerate yourself. So don't blame them. Admit your error, modify your behaviour and move on.

39 GIVE PRAISE WHERE PRAISE IS DUE – FOR EFFORT AS WELL AS ACHIEVEMENT

As a general rule, when the people for whom you are responsible do badly, you should let any blame fall on yourself and not them. But when they do well, you should make sure that any praise falls on them and not you.

Some managers like to give praise very publicly, in salesman-of-the-month mode. This is not always appropriate, and you have to be careful when praising people publicly that praise of one person is not seen as unwonted criticism of another. In general, though, for a manager as for a teacher, praise is one of the most powerful tools you have to motivate people to perform better and to make them feel positive about their work.

Praise operates at two levels. At one level, it is simply about acknowledging people's efforts and achievements. There is nothing more galling than to put yourself out and make a special effort, or to complete a tricky or challenging task, and to feel that it is not noticed or is taken for granted. People like their efforts and achievements, however modest, to be appreciated, and get grumpy when they're not. A simple acknowledgement spurs them to keep on trying and to keep on improving. A lack of acknowledgement and they ask themselves why they bother.

How much praise you give and in what way will depend on the person concerned, but in most cases it can be given in private, not in public, and so easily adapted to the person and the situation. Some people get uncomfortable if your praise is too fulsome, and respond better to a brief acknowledgement. Others need more pampering. Some need tokens of some kind, though gold stars and certificates are generally best kept for young children, not adults. As you get to know the people who work for you, you should find out how best to approach each one. The key thing, though, is to notice what they're doing – both what they are achieving and how much of an effort they are making, together with any challenges they are having to overcome in the process (difficult situations, other people, their own home concerns and so on) – and not let anything worthy of praise pass completely unnoticed.

At another level, praise can be used to channel people's efforts and personal and professional development in particular directions. Sometimes you might want to praise them for things for which they weren't expecting praise, because they didn't realize they were important or relevant to their jobs. Again, you might withhold praise for something while praising something else, not because the first thing wasn't good, but because you want to focus on the importance of the second. (In line with the principle of giving praise where it's due, you should generally withhold praise for one thing only when you can give it for another.)

You can also use public praise of one person to give messages to others. If some people aren't pulling their weight, or aren't pulling in the right direction, make a point of publicly praising those who are. Show through your praise what qualities you appreciate, as a manager, and what qualities the organization appreciates. Many organizations unwittingly operate a kind of caste system, where certain groups of people are culturally under-appreciated relative to others: clerical and junior administrative staff in a university or hospital, for example, or 'support' staff in a professional firm. This is usually a relic of history and not something that the organization desires, and the best way to address it is by praising these people in front of others – not singling them out, so much as making it plain that their achievements are of equal standing.

Everything that applies to the praise of individuals also applies to the praise of teams. The achievements of your unit may well be as much a function of how people work together as of how they work individually, and while you can recognize and direct team perform-ance partly through individual praise, the most appropriate focus of praise will often be the team itself. This is especially so in a public setting. Teamwork is a social activity. It is easier to draw attention to its qualities in a social setting, where you can focus people on the desirability of effective teamwork in general (regardless of the

Example 18: Responsibility and Praise

To some extent, the skills and attitudes required to manage people well either come naturally or they don't. So some people, reading through this part of the book, will just think, 'What a lot of tosh!' Those people shouldn't be managing at all. Brad the builder did some work for a property developer, Brian, who treated his own small team of personal assistants and handymen as if they were absolute rubbish. He was forever blaming them for not doing what he wanted but seemed incapable of praising them or of giving them any responsibility, and was completely deaf to any suggestions they might make. The strange thing was that while he was a sharp enough dealer and good enough networker to have got very rich, Brian seemed to be utterly miserable.

In fact there are many people who manage their own businesses but don't really manage the people they employ at all. Few are quite as abusive as Brian, but when it is the business, or just the profit, that matters to them, the people in it are sometimes treated as a nuisance or just ignored. And while few of these owner-managers are quite as miserable as Brian, few of them really enjoy what they are doing. Brad's approach to his business was quite different, for two main reasons. First, he wanted to create a business he could be proud of, not just something that would earn him money or even give him status. Second, he just didn't like being surrounded by people who were themselves unhappy or unfulfilled, and he didn't like being shut off and isolated from people either. So he really had no option but to try and manage. And the more he tried, the more rewarding he found it.

The main people challenge for Brad, as for many owner-managers, was letting go enough to devolve responsibility. He had a trusted number two, Bruce, whom he had known for many years, but he had only taken him on when his wife, Betty, had complained that a father really had to spend more time with his children than he was managing – that he had to manage at home, as well as at work. In fact, Bruce had made an enormous difference, and with the two of them to oversee things, they were able to build the business much better than he would have been on his own. Last summer, however, Bruce had had to go to Australia for an unknown period (it turned out to be ten weeks) to be with his terminally ill mother. The firm was the busiest it had ever been, and with two small children and a babe in arms, Betty was struggling too.

The situation looked impossible, but it was again Betty who suggested the answer: what about Bill? Bill was a young joiner who had been with the firm about three years and showed considerable promise. He had a positive attitude, maturity beyond his years and a good eye for detail. It happened that the joinery requirements of current jobs were manageable: some of the work could safely be contracted out and at least half of Bill's time could be freed up. It was not an easy call – Bill was still inexperienced and Brad was nervous – but he took the plunge.

The result? There were mistakes. Not everything went smoothly. But nor did anything disastrous happen. By the time Bruce returned, Bill had learnt a lot and was even more motivated than he had been. And Brad knew he had someone who could be trained up for the future, and knew what bits needed working on. Bill would probably end up with his own firm, maybe even as a competitor, but he would be an honest and fair competitor and Brad didn't mind that. At the end of the stint he praised him publicly and then told him privately not to get ahead of himself and to concentrate on his peer relationships.

In a very different situation, Belle would love to delegate more responsibility and is sure that several of her staff could benefit from it, but she doesn't have the scope to do it. In a large, bureaucratic organization, such as a retail bank, people's roles are very tightly defined. To a large extent, indeed, the branch manages itself or, at least, is managed as much by established rules and procedures as it is by people. What Belle has found, however, is that in this context, very little things can make a very big difference. Leaving someone to get on with a task, whereas before she had closely monitored them, is tantamount to devolving responsibility.

Something similar applies when it comes to giving praise. Belle is one of those people who not only appreciates the work of other people, but is very ready to show it. She's reluctant to talk about her own achievements – indeed, she's reluctant to talk about herself at all. She'd much rather sing other people's praises. This means, however, that a certain level of praise is taken for granted by her staff, and in the context of a bank in which everything personal tends to be understated but every word is carefully noted, she's learnt to fine-tune her comments – not only to pick her words carefully, but also to modulate the way she says them, to get the right messages across.

make-up of the team), rather than on the work of a particular team (with its particular interpersonal characteristics).

Finally, while praise can be a useful way of motivating people to meet and exceed their performance targets (the very public praise dished out in a classic American sales bash is a good example of this), it may be particularly important in motivating people along dimensions that are not incorporated into the formal performance measurement system. If, for example, the performance measurement system of an organization is based around individual incentives, giving praise for collegiality and teamwork may be especially important. Similarly, if the performance measurement system only recognizes the work of a group or team, you may want to pay particular attention to praising the efforts and achievements of individuals.

40 SEEK OUT, PROMOTE AND LEARN FROM PEOPLE WHO ARE BETTER THAN YOU

One of the challenges many managers find difficult is managing people who are in some way better than they are themselves: more talented, harder working, greater achievers and so on. This doesn't happen in every setting, but in most organizations it does. The best people have to work their way up, and on the way up they are bound to work at some point for people who are less able than they are. In very much the same way, academically strong children will inevitably be taught by teachers who are academically less gifted than they are. You may well think that you are better than your own manager, and you may be justified in thinking that, but you are not unique! Members of your own staff may well feel the same about you, and they may be justified too.

This can feel very threatening. Having someone below you whom you know is capable of identifying and criticizing your own weak points is not always comfortable, and some managers respond by protecting themselves from it. If they recognize people in their units who are a threat in this way, they put them down, both to their colleagues and to their own superiors, so as to neutralize the force of any potential criticism. If they see them as candidates for appointment, they dismiss them as unsuited to the job in question, whatever their qualities. If they manage to rise to middle or senior management positions in which they can, to some extent, pick and choose who works for them from within the organization, they choose people who will not be a threat over those who might be.

This is a very bad way to go about things. At a personal career level, it sometimes works. There are many organizations run by third-rate chief executives who have appointed fourth-rate senior management teams. They don't tend to last long, however, for obvious reasons, and when they do – in some well-protected public sector bureaucracies, for example – they consistently under-perform. Not only are the management teams weak, but anybody with any talent quickly gets out and goes elsewhere.

Of course, no one can admit to this. So the situation can only be sustained by a fiction, and the fiction that sustains these people is that they really are the best, not third-raters but first-raters. This starts out as a defensive justification for rejecting people who are better than they are, but they soon come to believe it. So, judging people by their own standards, they really do believe not only that they are first (not third) rate, but that their management teams are second (not fourth) rate.

This is sad, and if we accept the principles that nobody is perfect and that everyone has a particular mix of talents, competences and limitations, it is quite unnecessary. If you are a manager, the fact that someone who works for you, or who wishes to work for you, is quite probably more talented than you are, is something to be welcomed, not feared. Use them well and the performance of your unit will benefit. Support them and promote them, and you may find that they get a job that you wanted yourself – OK, but they will be grateful for your honest support and you will also have the opportunity to learn from them along the way. If you take that opportunity, you too will end up achieving much more than you would have done without them. In the long term it is a win–win situation.

So seek these people out, and when you find them, support them. Admit that they have qualities that you don't. There will always be other areas where you have skills or experience that they don't, so like the teacher of academically strong children, teach them what you can. And learn from them what you can. Even if they don't stay long, your unit will out-perform and, if you stick with the policy, you will build a reputation not only as a good manager yourself, but also as a mentor of managerial talent. And since their talents and their relative superiority will probably be quite apparent to everyone else (something that the managers who shun such competition typically overlook), you will earn far more respect from everyone if you admit to them, than if you deny them.

41 BE TOLERANT OF DISAGREEMENT AND IDIOSYNCRASY

Just as some managers will put down and hold back anybody who

Example 19: Valuing People

In a busy general hospital, Melanie is surrounded by personal differences: differences of ethnic and cultural background, of education and training, of values and beliefs. Idiosyncrasies abound. And looking around the hospital, she can see all sorts of responses to this. In some units, difference is strongly suppressed. In others, people are allowed to express themselves freely, but with unproductive consequences: persistent stand-offs between opposing views or the chaos of a free-for-all. Getting the right balance is evidently not easy. A particular challenge for matrons, like herself, is the persistent shortage of hospital nurses and the reliance, as a result, on agency staff. Sometimes agency nurses bring valuable new perspectives or new experiences, but move on too quickly for them to have any effect. Sometimes they can be positively disruptive and stay long enough for this to do damage. Melanie does her best to recognize and endorse what's valuable, while keeping a lid on what isn't, but in this respect she's still more coping than controlling.

Melanie also gets a glimpse of how different managers in the hospital respond when presented with staff more capable than themselves. She can see proactive, first-rate doctors stuck in units where consultants are resistant to change or just want a quiet life. And she can see other units that positively seek out and encourage the best talent, only to lose it quickly when consultancy jobs come up elsewhere.

Ed's challenge, when it comes to managing disagreement, is quite different. In a somewhat old-fashioned engineering firm, the main problem is that he doesn't have enough of it. Most people, including himself, are stuck in much the same mindset. We shall use Ed's situation in Chapter 6 to explore the kinds of techniques that can be used to open up ways of thinking about the future and, at the same time, to develop talent in the firm, so set that aside for now. He has also encountered the problem of managing people

is better than them, others will put down and hold back anybody who disagrees with them or who fails to conform to their preferred norms. These managers don't like being challenged or questioned, so they try to suppress anybody who challenges or questions them. They brook no disagreement and treat idiosyncrasy as insolence. Some managers are very forceful in the process, openly ostracizing

better than himself. Early in his career he was badly held back by a manager who felt threatened by his ability, gave him no scope to prove himself and gave consistently lukewarm appraisal reports. Later on he found himself managing someone who challenged him directly on an important commercial decision.

At that time Ed still thought he could make it to the top and was angling for a promotion. An issue had arisen and, seeking to advance his case, he had taken a stand. One of the young men reporting to him, Frank, had disagreed with his assessment and, after much debate, some of it quite tense, Ed had had to concede that he was right. After some soul-searching he had done the 'right thing', changed his recommendation and credited Frank with the analysis behind the change. Frank was in due course promoted above Ed, and then moved on to head up another firm in a slightly different field, but they remain in touch and each uses the other as a sounding board for their problems.

One of the ways Ed now makes use of these various experiences is in overseeing the way the sectional managers, who report directly to him, manage their own teams. From where he stands it's quite hard to see how well they're devolving responsibility, seeking out talent, giving praise when it's due, dealing with conflicts and niggles, and so on. For the most part he just has to trust them to take responsibility for this aspect of managing, as well as for the specific tasks of their sections. He can get some insights, however, by reviewing with them their staff appraisals. (In some organizations, appraisals are conducted by people other than line managers and the reports are strictly confidential, but this is now quite rare, and probably has more disadvantages than advantages.) He could treat this review process, as many managers do, as just a paper exercise, but Ed likes to go through the appraisal reports in face-to-face meetings with his team. He finds that the ways they respond to his questions tell him a lot, not only about the staff appraised but also about the appraisers and their management approaches.

people who don't fit in and actively punishing disagreement. Others are more subtle but still make it clear that these behaviours are not acceptable.

This kind of managerial intolerance may arise from an authoritarian disposition or a deep commitment to the qualities of obedience and conformity. It may equally arise from insecurity and a fear of criticism. Either way, it is a serious obstacle to effective management.

There is a time and place for disagreement. If members of your staff keep disagreeing for the sake of it, or voice their disagreement in an aggressive manner or at inappropriate times, or keep voicing their disagreement after matters have been fully aired and resolved, you may have to explain to them that their behaviour is unproductive and unhelpful. For a unit to work effectively there must be a pragmatic acceptance of the chosen policies and agreement on the actions required. Once decisions are taken, you can reasonably expect people to accept those decisions and get on with things, at least until such time as it is appropriate to revisit the issues concerned.

You can't expect everybody to agree with every decision, however. As in any political accommodation, there will inevitably be underlying and unresolved differences, and it would be very unhealthy if there were not. The existence of competing viewpoints means that there is somewhere to turn if the agreed policy doesn't work or if changes in the environment make it no longer appropriate. And the existence of critical minds keeps everybody on their toes and up to scratch. You may not want people to keep airing their disagreements, whether with you or with other members of their teams, but you do want to retain some contrasting views, and to retain the potential for disagreement.

It is also important, when you are taking decisions off your own bat, perhaps under pressure and with relatively little time for consultation, that you have people around who are prepared to disagree with you, to question your assumptions, challenge your logic or point out things you may have missed. And it is important for the organization that it contains people who are prepared to disagree with actions that might be unethical or in breach of regulations or other commitments. Again, you will want them to exercise discretion in how and when they voice that disagreement, but you won't want to lose the disagreement itself. If everyone agrees, then everybody is probably blinkered by the same set of prejudices.

So you should welcome an element of healthy disagreement and use it to good effect. And the same goes for idiosyncrasy. Don't dismiss people because they are different or pressure them to conform, because difference is a valuable resource. Different backgrounds, different cultures, different attitudes all enhance the skills, experience and ideas on which your unit can draw. Even the odd-balls bring something valuable that other people don't, with their unusual ways of looking at things. Indeed, the weirdest people are often the most creative. So don't think someone's odd, just think they're different and find ways of using the extra scope of potential that that difference brings.

42 GET PEOPLE MOVING IN THE SAME DIRECTION

Leadership, you will recall, is about lining people up and getting them all to pull in the same direction. And you may well ask how that squares with welcoming diversity, to the point of idiosyncrasy and disagreement. How can you hope to line people up if at the same time you're encouraging them to differ and disagree?

In essence, the situation is much the same as if you were managing a football team. A football team will include players with widely differing skills and characteristics – very widely differing, if you think of rugby or American football, where the different positions require very different combinations of speed, strength and agility. A top team is also likely to include some very strong characters, with strong opinions. The most brilliant talents can also be the most mercurial and idiosyncratic, and, in some cases, plain difficult. The strength of the team relies on these individual qualities, but it also relies on everyone playing together and committing to the same game plan, whatever they may think about it.

As in football management, success in management involves a balance between giving a group of diverse and free-thinking individuals free reign to employ their skills and talents, and persuading them to adapt and meld those skills and talents to the needs and chosen direction of the unit as a whole. This always entails some element of compromise. You coach the players to execute the plan, but you also adapt the plan to suit the players, and you accept that the result can never be perfect. You can very rarely get everyone to move in perfect alignment in precisely the direction you want.

The temptation in this situation is to stick to your chosen direction and just accept that people may not be fully lined up behind it. The theoretical plan is what is most in your control, so that is where you start. But a plan is only ever as good as its execution, and as in football, so in management: there is no point having a plan or a strategy if the players can't or won't stick to the roles you assign them. You are much better off pursuing a strategy that is, in theory, only second-best, but can be really well-executed. In other words, it is much better to have everyone moving in the same direction, even if that direction is slightly off from where you would like it to be. As in battle, the first priority is to hold your troops together and committed to the cause. The choice of tactics comes second.

How you get people aligned is really the subject of this whole book. You earn their respect and build their trust. You listen and learn about their own priorities and inclinations. You learn what motivates them and build incentives around that. You get a sense of where you can take them and where you can't. Someone once described leadership as watching where people are going and walking in front of them. That is clearly not enough. All organizations have their aims and purposes; your job, as a manager, is to steer your unit in the direction required. But steering people is more like herding animals than like steering a car. You have to be sensitive to the feedback you get when you push in different directions. You have to be aware of the direction people are going in and, to some extent, you do have to go with it, to walk in front of where people are going, to work with the flow rather than against it. Sometimes you can't get people from A to B in one go, but you can get them from A to C, then bend them round towards B and finally set their sights on B. If you watch an expert shepherd herding sheep, you will see that they often take quite a circuitous route in order to keep the flock together and prevent it scattering.

People are, on the whole, much more responsive than sheep, but they are also much more prone to scattering, and once they've scattered, it's the devil's job to get them back together again. So the priority is even more to hold them together.

43 BE INTOLERANT OF BULLYING, LYING OR SELFISH SUBVERSION

Tolerance of diversity and idiosyncrasy is undoubtedly a good thing for a manager, even if it sometimes makes life more difficult – but there are limits. These are essentially moral limits, and they relate particularly to unethical behaviours that do damage to the organization, the unit and the people in the unit.

Everyday morality is rarely a black and white issue. Everybody has their own, slightly different, moral standards, and it is not generally part of a manager's job to say what these should be, especially if they don't impinge directly on work.

You can certainly encourage people to be kind, courageous, compassionate, dutiful or generous; to turn the other cheek when attacked and not to dissemble when in a fix. But you have to accept that people exercise these virtues in different measures and in different ways. You have to accept too that different people will balance or prioritize their duties in different ways, leading to different levels of commitment to work and home, colleagues and organization, and so on. If important duties are being neglected, you should say

or do something, but there is a wide range of perfectly acceptable behaviours within which these are simply matters of personal
choice.

In most organizations, this even applies to things like the use
of work time and facilities. Clearly, people should not steal things
from work or abuse any freedom they are given, and if they do,
then you will have to act. But the guidelines for the private use of
telephones or email are usually open to interpretation, and so long
as people are behaving reasonably responsibly and not neglecting
their work, interfering with other people's work or intentionally
stealing, some latitude is often appropriate.

The ways people behave out of work are also, for the most part,
not your business. If somebody on your staff is cheating on his wife,
you may strongly disapprove, but it is not for you to interfere.

Where you should interfere is where someone's behaviour is
clearly unethical and clearly impacts adversely either on the work
of the organization or on the people for whom you are responsible.
And you should be especially vigilant with regard to behaviours
that, while they might do relatively little damage to start off with,
become very damaging if allowed to continue.

The most obvious example of such a behaviour is bullying. Bullying typically starts in a little way and gradually builds, as the bully
gains confidence and satisfaction, and the person bullied grows
more fearful and more vulnerable. If allowed to continue it becomes
institutionalized, in the sense that both sides take it for granted
and don't even think of it as bullying. It just becomes built in to
the relationship they have. In time the victims do not even think of
themselves as victims. But they are victims, and the damage done to
them is immense. They are hurt, emotionally, and disabled, practically, from fulfilling their potential. And, though this is a secondary
consideration, the organization suffers too. Neither party contrib-
utes what they could, their relationships with other colleagues
suffer and an appalling example is set.

Managers can be reluctant to act on bullies, partly because they
are themselves a bit scared of them and partly because bullying can
be very difficult to prove (even the person bullied, if sufficiently
cowed, will often deny it). Bullying only gets worse if it's allowed
to develop, however, so the best policy is one of zero tolerance.
If you suspect that it is going on, act immediately to support the
person being bullied and make your concerns clear to the suspected
bully. You don't have to accuse them: harassment is defined as
the experience of feeling harassed and in the initial stage you are
merely bringing that person's feelings to people's attention. If they

are innocent, talking will flush out whatever the problem is. If they are guilty, they might well accuse you of harassing them. Too bad, that's a risk you have to take, and most well-run organizations are quite capable of protecting you if needed.

Closely related to bullying, another example is where people distort the work of a team or unit to meet their own selfish needs. They might, for example, misrepresent the work of a team so as to claim credit for themselves, while denigrating the work of their colleagues, even if those colleagues did all the work. They might be uncooperative, if they see nothing personally to be gained by cooperation. Or they might redirect the aim of a project from what best serves the organization to what best serves their own careers.

Like bullying, this harms both colleagues and the organization. It doesn't fall under formal procedures for harassment, so is not really a disciplinary matter, but it is a matter of work perform-

---

Example 20: Freedom, Direction and Necessary Constraints

When it comes to managing people, Polly's challenges are as great as anybody's. If she couldn't tolerate idiosyncrasy and disagreements amongst her school staff, she wouldn't be able to do her job. Most of her teachers have strong views on how children should be taught and how schools should be run. They often disagree sharply and one or two of them, while extremely gifted in particular ways, are borderline mad.

In this context, one of Polly's big challenges is to get people lined up and moving in roughly the same direction; this requires compromise. It requires compromise on her part, because the direction on which agreement is achievable is not quite what she would have chosen, given a completely free hand. And it requires compromises on the teachers' parts. This is made much easier, Polly finds, if she is generous with her praise and restrained in her criticism. If she criticizes a teacher's approach, however constructively, the teacher will tend to dig her heels in when it comes to agreeing and implementing a school-wide policy. If she praises what the teachers achieve, they will tend to be less defensive about their approaches and more willing to accommodate adjustments. By emphasizing the positive she builds up mutual respect between the teachers, and this then acts as a basis for reasonable compromises.

Respect matters a lot to Polly, and whether it is because of this, or

ance, so there is no need for reticence in giving your opinions as a manager. Move quickly, support anybody who is suffering from the behaviour and communicate your own impressions to the person concerned. Knowing that you are watching, they will either stop playing that particular game or try and move to a unit where they can get away with it more easily – but for that, of course, they will need your reference.

A third example is lying. Like bullying, lying is insidious. Little lies, if you allow people to get away with them, lead on to bigger lies. They don't always do personal harm and there might be no ill-intent. Compulsive liars often see no harm in what they are doing, and may even be fantasists, oblivious to the fact that they are lying. Because not everyone will be in a position to recognize their lies as lies, however, they can play havoc with the work of your unit. They can also do a lot of unintentional harm, as people base their judge-

---

because of her experiences of children, or just because of circumstances, she is one of only two of our managers to have picked up a case of staff bullying. (The other is Rick, who is constantly struggling with bullying in both the kitchens and front of house. In a busy restaurant, the pressures to deliver with almost military precision lead easily to a control culture, which can very easily slide into harassment.) The class concerned ran well, the teaching was good and there were no complaints from parents or staff. But something alerted her to the fact that in a school in which disagreements were commonplace, the class assistants seemed just a bit too subservient. And when she looked back at the records she was surprised to find that nobody starting as a teaching assistant in that class had ever gone on to take a class of their own. They just stayed a few years then left. It was a difficult one because the assistants at first denied that anything was wrong and there was no overt harassment but, by carefully probing, she eventually discovered the teacher concerned had long been emotionally manipulating and controlling her assistants, more, it seemed, out of a simple desire for power than anything else. Then, when she got bored, she would effectively discard them, telling them they had no future in the school and encouraging them to leave. Which was more or less the message Polly gave the teacher who, her game ruined, just moved on. Where or how, Polly never knew: she only once gave a reference, very carefully worded, and wasn't asked for one again.

144 FIFTY GUIDELINES FOR EFFECTIVE MANAGING

ments of other people upon false and misleading evidence. And once they spread beyond the unit – as they inevitably will – they can get it, you and the organization as a whole into serious trouble. Habitual liars, because they speak with great conviction and great freedom, are very often precisely the people who are thought by outsiders to be telling the truth about their organizations.

Because no-one is perfectly truthful, it can be hard to determine when lying becomes an issue. Whenever you get an indication that people are straying from the honest truth, however, you should immediately pick them up on what they say and question what they mean. Sometimes this in itself will be enough to curb their behaviour. But, even if it isn't, it will give you an insight into their behaviour and an indication of what to watch out for in the future. And if you do find people being blatantly dishonest, however unintentionally, you should immediately make it clear that that is unacceptable.

44 DEAL QUICKLY WITH CONFLICTS AND NIGGLES – DON'T LET THEM FESTER

Some issues, like bullying, need quick action because of their importance and their capacity for serious harm. Others need quick action precisely because they are unimportant. You just need to get them out of the way so that people can get on with what matters. Petty personal conflicts, minor irritations and niggles fall into this category.

If you throw a bunch of people together in a work situation, it is almost inevitable that some of them won't get on. Others, though they might rub along together well enough most of the time, will occasionally rub each other up the wrong way and get on each other's nerves. Even close friends, who have chosen to spend their time together for pleasure, have occasional spats or days when things don't click. Even families, who may not have chosen each other but who have a lot in common and a lot of shared experience on which to build, are prone to minor (or major) feuds.

People at work know that they have to spend time in each other's company and, by and large, they make the most of whatever that company is. But with all sorts of different backgrounds, experiences, attitudes, beliefs and personalities, they won't always rub along smoothly. Sometimes they will grate. One person may be irritated by another's attitudes or habits. Two people might vie for attention. People might disagree passionately about some trivial aspect of their jobs or about the allocation of space in the fridge or the position of a pot plant. They might get upset about minor disparities in their duties or rewards. A mother might be irritated by the need for meetings early or late in the day, while someone without home demands might be irritated by the mother's inflexibility, or even irritated by her irritation. If people are shy or awkward or just different, they might feel they're being left out of things, while everybody else feels that they're not joining in.

All these things are an unavoidable part of people working together. They also get in the way of people working together effectively. And while some of them only arise occasionally and pass quickly, others fester. What starts out as a very minor annoyance becomes a persistent source of irritation. What starts out as a simple difference of opinion turns into a prolonged stand-off. For the silliest of reasons, people find themselves emotionally drained and distracted from their work.

You may feel, as a manager, that you have much more important things to do than to get involved in people's petty squabbles, but the longer you leave these things, the harder it will be to deal with them, so it makes sense to act quickly. As soon as you see a problem emerging, get people together and get them to talk about it. Sometimes that will be enough on its own to restore harmony, or at least to stop things deteriorating, and get people focused back on their work. Sometimes you may have to act as adjudicator and take sides. Sometimes you may be unable to resolve what's at issue but still be able to set some limits: 'If you can't agree, so be it, but don't drag in other people'. There's no need to be authoritarian about it, but if you have people's respect and show some normal human sympathy and understanding, you should be able to impose some basic house rules, accepted as being in everybody's interests.

45 DON'T UNDERMINE PEOPLE OR CRITICIZE THEM IN PUBLIC – EVEN IF THEY DESERVE IT

It should by now be pretty obvious that good managers don't undermine their own staff or criticize them in public. We have repeatedly emphasized the positives of praise and support over the negatives of blame and public critique in this context, and the lesson should be easily learnt. It is sometimes more difficult to follow the same principles in respect of your peers and superiors.

As we have noted, you will often find yourself, if you are a good manager, working for, and with, people who are in some respects less good, who don't come up to your own standards or expectations. They may seem lazy or uncommitted to the organization. They may lack particular skills or talents that seem to be needed for the jobs they're doing. They may be the kinds of people we have just discussed: bullies, manipulators or liars. Or they may be the kinds of people we discussed earlier, who try to hide their own limitations by denying the skills and competences of others. They may just strike you as incompetent.

You will not normally be responsible for these people, in the way that you are responsible for the people who report to you, so you won't have the same duty of care. But you will have a responsibility to them, and also to the organization you all work for. And you may well feel that these clash, that their actions or inactions are damaging the organization and need to be addressed. When the issue is one of competence or judgement, you can address it simply by arguing a counter-position, in meetings or committees or through written reports, as appropriate. But when the issue is one of attitude or general ability – of work rate or commitment, of the way they go about their jobs or treat other people, of values or ethics – things get more difficult. You won't normally achieve anything by raising these issues with them, so the temptation will be to raise them with other people.

This is fine, within limits and so long as it's done in the right way. It is quite appropriate to express frustration to your manager, to a colleague or even sometimes to a more senior manager, that things are not going as you would wish. Remember, though, that what you are expressing is an opinion not a fact, that it is your particular and inevitably partial view of the situation and that other people may have other, equally valid, views. There may be personal circumstances or an organizational context that you know nothing about. It may well be that the situation is already being managed, but that this is being done confidentially, in a particular way and at a particular pace, for very good reasons that are nothing to do with you. You have to trust your senior managers, collectively if not individually, and if you can't trust them at all, you should probably be moving on.

The fact that your own view will always be partial and incomplete is also one reason – and a very important one – for not making your criticisms more public, either explicitly or implicitly. It is unfair to criticize people from a position of ignorance, and in this case you will always be in a position of relative ignorance. There are other reasons too. Those who live in glass houses shouldn't throw stones: whether you are aware of them or not, you will have your own weaknesses that will be equally vulnerable to critique. Nor is it ever wise to throw the first stone or, indeed, to strike back when hit. Internal discord can only harm an organization, and there are very few cases indeed when public criticism of a colleague or superior (public, that is, in the sense of public within part of the organization, never mind public beyond the organization) will be in the organization's interests. You may be fuming inside, but you must let patience and reticence prevail.

You must also be careful not to critique people implicitly, and undermine their positions, just by the way you talk about them. It is very easy to put people down and damage their reputations without even knowing you are doing it. A particular choice of words, a casual reference or disclaimer, a snide remark, a poorly chosen joke, a facial expression or an unconscious gesture can all speak volumes, and can do just as much harm as an outright accusation.

What are the exceptions to all this? When should you speak out? The most obvious cases are those of fraudulent behaviour, physical or sexual abuse, blatant discrimination and other plainly illegal acts. Even here you should be very careful – you may be mistaken and, even if you are not, you shouldn't normally go public unless you have satisfied yourself that senior managers can't or won't deal with the situation. Having said that, there is 'dealing with the situation' and 'dealing with the situation'. You have a duty to society and to humanity, as well as to your bosses, and it may be that that duty is overriding, even at the cost of your own job.

The most difficult thing to deal with is unethical behaviour that stops short of outright illegality: bullying, harassment, lying, favouritism and discrimination, and general unkindness. This has no place in organizational life, and because it causes serious emotional harm, it is hard for someone watching on to endure. Moreover, if you see someone as seriously immoral, you are likely to respond emotionally to anything they say or do and to get worked up about actions that are, in themselves, quite reasonable. You will instinctively want to distance yourself from them and, in so doing, you will easily find yourself undermining their position.

The best way to think about immorality is probably as a kind of moral incompetence, to be handled like any other form of incompetence – not, in other words, by publicly criticizing it. If, having brought your view of things to the attention of the appropriate person or people, in an appropriate way, nothing is done about it, you should probably just look for another job. The fault is unlikely to lie with any sympathy amongst senior management towards immorality, though that might be the case on specific culturally embedded issues, such as gender discrimination. It is much more likely to lie with their general weakness, with their inability to take the situation on rather than letting it drift. That is not something that you can address, publicly or privately.

Example 21: When to Keep Quiet

Like Ed, Belle has more difficulty generating disagreement than controlling it. Her bank branch is multi-racial and gender-mixed, and differences are easily accepted, but everybody is very respectful and any disagreements and personal idiosyncrasies are very mildly expressed. Her challenge is not so much to tolerate them as to quietly tease them out. At this level of the bank, personal honesty and mutual respect can be pretty well taken for granted, bullying is almost unheard of and open conflicts are rare. There are personal conflicts and niggles, however, as there are in most offices, and since they tend to be suppressed, they can be hard to manage. Belle often has to say things without actually saying them, and find roundabout ways to cut off possible sources of tension.

Within the bank hierarchy, Belle sits somewhere in lower middle management and this means that, unlike Brad or even, for the most part, Ed, she has to manage people upwards as well as downwards. In particular she has to deal with superiors who have not necessarily come up through the branch system and who, while no doubt very bright, don't necessarily understand how things work on the ground. A particular problem here is Boris, an assistant regional manager, who came into the bank on a fast-track graduate route and comes across, not to put too fine a point on it, as a bit of a pompous prat. Boris is not Belle's immediate boss but he quite often visits the branch for one thing or another. She knows that her staff take the Mickey when he does and she is sorely tempted to join in. She could have a good joke and give everyone a bit of fun, and he probably wouldn't even notice. Fortunately, she also knows that that's not the way to manage. Boris is probably very good at the technical side of his job and it's important that the people he works with in the branch respect him for that. His own manager will be working on the personal side, and anything Belle does or says can only make that person's job harder, not easier.

---

46 PROVIDE STABILITY – WELCOME CHANGE

One way of looking at the last few guidelines is to see them as providing the stability that your unit needs to get its work done effectively. This stability comes from being able to live comfortably with difference and variety; being free from the worries of having to cope with bullies, liars and egoists; being free from the disruptive effects of persistent interpersonal conflicts and niggles; and knowing that their manager is not going to get them into trouble by rocking the boat with colleagues and bosses.

Stability is important because it enables people to concentrate on the job in hand and provides a sound footing when they have to tackle unexpected events. If they don't have a sound footing, all their efforts will go into coping and surviving, and anything that threatens to disrupt them further will either blow them over completely or just be ignored. One of your most important functions as a manager, then, is to protect your unit from sources of instability, both external and internal, to keep it on an even keel, poised and ready to respond to whatever it needs to, from whatever direction.

Stability is also important, ironically, because it provides a platform for change. Change is always threatening. Whatever they may say to the contrary, many people are uneasy, or even frightened, at the prospect of having to change established habits, face unknown challenges and generally move out of their comfort zones. Faced with unfamiliar situations, they are always tempted to fall back on what's familiar, even if it's quite inappropriate. Managing change, accordingly, is partly about forcing people to break with their past habits, and some of our guidelines have already addressed this. We have noted, for example, that when leading change, you need to create new stories to replace the old ones and to engage people in those stories, to establish them firmly in their minds.

Change is much more threatening, however, and so much more difficult, when people start out feeling insecure. If they have a stable and secure starting point, people will generally be much more willing to take risks. They will feel – or will convince themselves – that they have a kind of lifeline or a safe haven they can return to in the event of trouble. As a manager you may well wish, once the journey is under way, to deny them that safe haven, but it is still psychologically important, and it will remain so until a new haven, a new stable state, can be reached.

So providing stability and welcoming change – and encouraging other people to welcome it too – are not as they might seem opposites, but complements and, as a manager, you should always be doing both. You first provide the stability that gives people the confidence to entertain change and to be open to seeing it as an opportunity or an adventure, not a threat. You then encourage them to think that way, to open their minds to new possibilities and to welcome new initiatives.

47 BE POSITIVE, BE FRIENDLY, BE COURTEOUS

For the last group of guidelines we turn back to your personal behaviour and attitude to the job, and to some general principles that really apply whatever job you're in, whether or not you're a manager, but are especially important in the management context.

Be positive, be friendly, be courteous. Courtesy is sometimes seen as an old-fashioned virtue that has perhaps gone out of fashion, but a lack of courtesy is both selfish and unproductive, and what really changes is not courtesy itself but the way it is shown. If you are a man, then one sign of courtesy in the past would have been to hold doors open for women. Nowadays that gender-based behaviour may or may not be appropriate (it probably depends on the woman) but there's no reason why you shouldn't hold a door open for anybody. And there is no reason why you shouldn't address anyone, whoever they are, with politeness and evident respect, behave in little ways to make them feel more comfortable, and remember and act on the little things that matter to them: how they like to be addressed, what tends to upset them, how they take their tea.

You may feel that, in an organizational context, you are more important than the people who work for you, but in human terms no-one is more important than anyone else. As a manager you could probably get away with things you couldn't otherwise. If you are rude to your staff, for example, they will probably have to put up with it. But why be rude? Even if you have to discipline or admonish someone, there is never any need, or any excuse, for rudeness.

In practical terms, courtesy also brings benefits. People are much more likely to do what you ask if you ask them nicely. Angry outbursts may help you let off steam, but they are generally counter-productive. So stay polite and let off steam somewhere else. Or, if you really can't help yourself, apologize afterwards. People also look to their managers to set an example, so courtesy on your part begets courtesy in others, leading to a more stable, more harmonious and more productive work environment.

Much the same applies to friendliness. To be friendly is to start any interpersonal exchange, or to hear anything about a person, from an assumption of sympathy and a desire to understand. It is to start out by assuming the best you reasonably can of people and to show this assumption in your speech and behaviour. It is not to be unrealistic about their faults. We know full well that even our best friends have faults, as we do ourselves, and one of the markers of true friendship is that it survives that knowledge. But we also try to help our friends erase their worst faults and to protect them, and others, from their effects. So too at work. If someone has an ethical weakness or a behavioural problem, you should try and address it as a friend would, and not just condemn it as if they were an enemy.

Friendliness is catching, so being friendly yourself will result in a friendlier unit, in which people are readier and more able to come to each other's aid. And being friendly towards everyone, as a matter of policy, counters the risk that you might be unintentionally discriminating by being friendly towards the people you just happen to like or get on with, and not towards those you don't. It helps you to treat people fairly and equally.

The virtues of being positive are perhaps slightly less obvious. Some people are naturally optimists and others pessimists. Some people see a glass half full, while others see it half empty, and a tendency towards pessimism or negativity doesn't normally carry the moral connotations of a tendency toward rudeness or hostility. But negativity can be very harmful and it is, at least partly, within your control. As a general rule, people always perform better when they look at things in a positive light, and this is certainly true of managers.

Like depression, which is its pathological cousin, negativity is disabling and enervating. It prevents you from getting on with things. Unlike clinical depression, however, it is controllable. So to get things done you put the negatives to one side and seek out the positives. You look on the bright side. You don't ignore the problems – it is a positive attitude to reality you are seeking, not a Utopian fantasy – but you focus on the solutions. And like friendliness and courtesy, that communicates itself to your staff, and encourages them to address problems positively, not just wallow in them.

48 ENCOURAGE HAPPINESS, BRING JOY

'OK', you may think, 'I can see why being positive might make me a better manager, but encouraging happiness, bringing joy? Is that really part of my job?' – yes, it is! If I had to select just one management truth, it would be that people work best when they are happy in their work.

The litmus test for this is how people feel when they arrive at their place of work. All too often their hearts sink as they walk through the door and don't lift up again until they leave. They may put on a cheerful face and may even feel cheerful momentarily when something happens to take them out of their gloomy selves. But really they're just going through the motions, and that carries over from their general demeanour to the work they do. If people aren't happy at work, they tend to just go through the motions of work, to get through their tasks but not to engage with them or put in the effort that is needed to do a really good job.

If, on the other hand, people's spirits lift up when they walk through the door, because they are happy to be at work and look forward to enjoying the day, they will tend to work well. They will give work that extra attention, put in that extra effort. They will help out their colleagues and pull together in a crisis.

There are qualifications, of course. The happiness has to come from doing the work and not from avoiding it. But by and large people who avoid work, or whose jobs make few demands on them, are not happy. It may be great for a few weeks, but they quickly get bored, listless and dissatisfied. People like to be busy and are generally happiest when they are.

So what can you do as a manager to make people happy? Many of the things we've covered in these guidelines help, from trusting people and treating them with respect to removing sources of tension and creating a positive, low-stress environment; and from doing your own administration conscientiously, to explaining carefully what you expect of people. Explaining why their work matters and how it adds value is also very important. This is much easier in some settings than others: easier in a school, for example, than in a warehouse. But all jobs add value to somebody in some way; if they didn't, they wouldn't exist. And if you remind people that their jobs are worthwhile, that also reminds them that they are worthwhile, and makes happiness easier to achieve. The most important thing, though, is to show people that you care about their happiness, that it matters to you.

This is where joy comes in. The Buddhists have a virtue called 'sympathetic joy', which is roughly speaking about rejoicing in other people's achievements and sharing the pleasure these bring. If people are sad, you should be compassionate and caring, and you should do what you can to make them happy. If they are happy, you should revel in their happiness, and palpably so. Smile and the whole world smiles with you.

49 MANAGING IS AN ART: PRACTICE, LEARN, IMPROVE

The joy of managing would be a fitting place to end these guidelines. Done well, and in a supportive and constructive environment, it can be a great joy, and one of the most satisfying and rewarding things you could ever do in life. But it is not always a joy and, even when it is, you have to work at it. So we'll finish this part of the book with some simple guidelines for when the going gets tough.

Managing is an art. Anyone can do it, just as anyone can paint, draw or play notes on a piano. But doing it well is another matter. If you are unusually gifted, you might be able to paint pictures or play the piano to a reasonable level of competence with minimal tuition. There are still things you need to learn, however, and most people will need to study, whether from a book or with a teacher. This book is indeed a kind of self-help study guide for managing.

You will also need to practice. You wouldn't expect to get very far with playing the piano if you didn't practice (well, you might expect to, but your teacher wouldn't expect you to and, in this case, the teacher would be right!) and the same is true of managing. You might think, if you are employed as a manager, that your whole day is spent practising, but unless you consciously attend to it, it won't be. There is a difference between spending an hour hitting the keys of a piano and spending an hour practising scales and tunes, and there is a difference between 'being a manager' and 'practising managing'. You need to think consciously about what you're doing and closely monitor the outcomes.

Practising in this sense is closely linked to learning. We learn how to do things through a process of feedback. Pianists listen to the sound they make, experiment with how to make a better sound, and learn the techniques and approaches that work best. In managing, your feedback comes from your performance, from your unit's performance, and from the responses you get from your staff and from your own managers. To learn, you need to reflect and act on those responses, constantly asking yourself how you could do better.

And you can, always, do better. Just as even the greatest pianists keep practising, learning and improving their playing, so do the best managers. And for ordinary managers, like you or me, there is plenty of room for improvement! Moreover, because every situation you encounter as a manager is different, you will need to keep learning just to keep up your performance level. Every new person you are responsible for, every new situation you face and every new organization you work for presents you with a new set of challenges.

50 A JOB IS JUST A JOB – DON'T GET IT OUT OF PERSPECTIVE

The forty-nine guidelines so far have been based on the importance of managing and the rewards it can bring, both to you and to the

Example 22: Last Words

The last few sections have been as much about attitudes as about behaviours, so let's close by asking what our managers would say about their experiences of managing. In order of appearance:

George 'The best experience of my life. It's made me what I am.' (Can you expand a bit?) 'I think the things that make for a good manager are more or less the same things that make for a good person. For me, the responsibility of managing at work was just what I needed to become more responsible at managing my life. I grew with the job, so to speak. Now, for other people it might be different. They might bring the skills they develop in their home lives and their social lives into managing at work. But for me it was the other way around.'

Melanie 'Well the first thing to say is that there's so much joy to be found on a maternity ward that you can't not share in it. But my first matron's post was on a cancer ward and I have to say there was something like joy there too. What I learnt there was how rewarding it is to help people help other people, and what enormous scope there is everywhere for doing things better. Not that they were done badly at all – don't get me wrong – but no organization is perfect. You can always find ways to give a better service. I'm not sure I'd want to be in senior management. The problems there are all to do with changing governance structures and increasing job pressures, and they're a long way away from the services that are actually delivered. But at my level you can just take that context as it is – no-one's going to reallocate funds on my say-so – and get on with the job of doing the best you can for the people you're serving. And that's immensely rewarding.'

Polly 'Phew! Ask me again in ten years! At this point I'd say frustrating and rewarding in equal measure. Sometimes it feels like you're banging your head against a brick wall, except that a brick wall is far too regular and even for the analogy to work. More like being banged on the head by the contents of a contemporary sculpture gallery. Then sometimes things seem to fall into place and you get this great positive adrenalin rush.

I moved into management basically because I was fed up with being badly managed, and that's still what motivates me: to create an environment in which my teachers can get on with doing really good things and the children can get all the benefits of that. I hadn't realized quite how challenging that would be, but now that I can see all the difficulties, I think it's even more important to overcome them. And I think I'm managing to do that, just about!'

Rick 'A great challenge. I've always liked projects and the restaurant gives me a new one every week! Seriously, though, the initial project of getting it up and going was fantastic. It was exhausting and maddening and at times impossible, but the feeling of achievement when it was done was just wonderful. Then after that I found it more of a grind: niggling problems, and the same ones over and over, but what I gradually realized was that keeping a place like this going – keeping the buzz, keeping the standards, keeping it profitable – is an even bigger project than setting it up. And then there are the staff. Most of them are pretty poorly paid and in the ordinary run of things they'd just drift from one job going nowhere to another. But there's so much hidden talent there if you go out looking for it! And as a manager you can make a difference with those people, help them make something of themselves. I doubt if I'll stay here more than a few years. I'd like to try something on my own, or try something really different like one of the big hotels, but I have to say that when I'm not tearing my hair out, I'm enjoying it.'

Ed 'I don't really know. It's a bit like asking a football player what's his experience of playing football. I'm a manager. I manage. And that's basically what I've done for most of my career. I always wanted to get ahead, so I applied for promotion, and with promotion came management. I still wanted to get ahead, so I practised my managing just like a footballer would practise his footballing, and I'll keep practising until I retire. I think I'm good at it, and I enjoy it. I like people, which helps. And I like doing things properly, which probably helps too. If I were still an engineer I'd try to design better machines. I'm a manager so I try to create better teams, a better company. Does that answer your question?'

(continued overleaf)

Brad 'My experience of managing? I don't think I see myself as a manager. I run a business.' (But you manage the business, you manage projects, you manage your workforce.) 'OK, I suppose so. Well, managing the business is very hard work and it's stressful and it makes my head hurt, but it's very satisfying because it's something I'd wanted to do and making a success of it is an achievement. Managing the projects, there Bruce helps me and I think we're pretty well on top of that, so there are always problems but they get solved and we deliver the goods, and you might get three months of angst but at the end of it there's a new building or a renovation and a satisfied customer – well, usually a satisfied customer – so that's rewarding and a source of pride. Managing the guys, that's probably what I've found hardest in some ways, because, as I say, I'm a builder not a manager, but you've got to do it and it's quite a buzz, actually, when someone pulls out the stops for you, or does something you didn't think he was capable of, or they all pull together and help each other out rather than hanging around waiting for each other, which is what builders usually do. So yes, it's good. It's ---- hard work, but good.'

people you manage. For your own health and well-being, however, it is essential that you don't overestimate its importance and get it out of perspective. Some organizations can put you under intolerable pressures to perform. Some bosses can be so maddeningly incompetent or unethical that you get hopelessly torn between what is demanded of you and what is right for the organization. Too many managers either get landed in positions of severe stress or land themselves in such positions and end up suffering heart attacks, strokes or mental breakdowns. Others get so absorbed in their jobs that they devote all their time and energy to them and none to their spouses or their children. Managing in an organization matters – it matters hugely. But it doesn't matter that much! It's not a life's vocation, to which everything else takes second place – it's a job.

This should be very obvious, but it's surprisingly easy to lose sight of it. Some people are very resistant to moving jobs. They don't like the uncertainty or the hassle of finding a new one, and there are times when it's not easy to find a new one, especially in a recession, where family commitments tie you to a particular location, where you work in a relatively narrow specialist field, or when you and your partner are both working and a move for one has impli-

Belle 'Well it's a good job, a good career, and it's manageable. Challenging without being too demanding. I wasn't sure about coming back to work after the children but, as it turned out, my husband's firm was taken over and he found himself with a boss who was just unmentionable – arrogant, self-centred, deceitful. And it was so stressful working under this guy, so eventually I said, "Just quit, it's not worth it: I can earn enough to keep us going while you find something else". And he did, and I'm so glad he did because I think he'd have had a heart attack otherwise. Anyway he did find another job, but by that time I was quite enjoying myself here. There are times when it gets really busy, but they're good employers, they're flexible when it comes to working round the children, and the staff are lovely. I suppose I manage them, but I can't say it's a great burden, more helping than managing. And it's nice when you see them do well and they get their promotions and you know you've played a teeny part in that. I suppose some people would prefer a job that's more exciting, but I get my excitement from white water rafting – that surprised you, didn't it! This suits me perfectly.'

cations for the other. Some people are very loyal to the organizations they work for and feel a duty to put up with the stresses of a bad manager or bad times, to keep fighting rather than desert. Some people just get very wrapped up in their jobs. They take their problems home with them and think about them night and day, impervious both to their own health and to the needs of family and friends. This is a particular risk in management jobs because they are effectively endless: they will take up as much time and attention as you will let them.

All these behaviours are quite understandable, but none is healthy. If you're good enough to be in a management role in the first place, you can probably find another job if you want to. It may not be in the ideal place or the ideal sector, but it will be better than being laid up in hospital. Loyalty to an organization is a good thing, but organizations aren't people. They constantly survive changes in personnel and your own organization won't suffer nearly as much from losing you as you think. Families, on the other hand, are different. If your preoccupations with work take you away from your partner or limit the love and attention you can give to your children, those relationships are not replaceable in the same way. At the end of the day, unless you are single and friendless (and with the exception of some jobs that are also vocations), letting your work rule your life is simply selfish in the short term and harmful, to you as well as to others, in the longer term.

When people write about this it is usually in terms of achieving a work–life balance, but that is slightly misleading. Work and life are not things to be balanced against each other, because life is much greater than work. Work has its part to play in how you live, as do other necessities like eating and drinking. But if you let work take over how you live, it will be a bit like building your life around meals: pleasurable or sickening, depending on the amount and the context, but no way healthy.

CHAPTER 4

Budgets, Costs and Financial Viability

Not every management role carries financial responsibility but many do, and even if yours doesn't, it still sometimes helps to have a grasp of the financial picture. To do this you need a basic grasp of accounting and finance. You don't need to be a trained accountant, nor do you need to be proficient in the mathematics of finance. All you really need to be able to do is to add and subtract, and to understand what it is that you're adding or subtracting. You should be able to read and write a simple budget, and to assess outcomes against a budget. Beyond this, you will find it helpful if you can also read a simple set of financial accounts and so get an idea of how your organization as a whole is performing. And you may also find it helpful if you can estimate the financial viability of a project or investment.

Most organizations have to prepare financial accounts on at least an annual basis, and most businesses and charities have to make public summaries of these accounts. The aim of these accounts is to

	2013-2014	2014-2015
Total income from sales	520,000	610,000
Food and drink	170,000	200,000
Wages and salaries	220,000	230,000
Rent, rates and insurance	55,000	55,000
Misc. services and supplies	76,000	90,000
Interest charges	3,000	3,000
Depreciation	11,000	11,000
Total expenditure	535,000	589,000
Profit / (loss)	(15,000)	21,000

Simple restaurant profit and loss account

	2013-2014	2014-2015
Total cash from sales	520,000	610,000
Food and drink	165,000	204,000
Wages and salaries	220,000	230,000
Rent, rates and insurance	55,000	55,000
Misc. services and supplies	76,000	90,000
Interest charges	3,000	3,000
Loan repayment		10,000
Total cash outflow	519,000	592,000
Net cash inflow (outflow)	1,000	28,000

Simple restaurant cash flow statement

give a 'true and fair' view of the financial state of the enterprise, and
in all but the smallest organizations they will generally be audited
by professional accountants to confirm that they do this. The main
elements of these financial accounts are: a Profit and Loss Account,
showing a breakdown of the income and expenditure for the year
and a resulting profit or loss figure; a Cash Flow Statement, showing
a breakdown of what cash came into and went out of the enterprise;
and a Balance Sheet, giving a summary of the assets and liabilities
of the enterprise and its residual value to shareholders or trustees.

The figure illustrates simplified versions of the Profit and Loss
Account, Cash Flow Statement and Balance Sheet for Rick's restaurant.

The Profit and Loss Account is your best guide to how the
organization has been faring recently, and is fairly self-explanatory.
Income will be listed under simple headings (sales, grants, donations, etc.) and expenditure similarly. Note that in a VAT-registered
business, all amounts shown will be exclusive of VAT.

In the case of the restaurant, there is only really one income source
– what the customers pay. There are various different expenditures, however, for food and drink, wages and salaries, advertising,
laundry, IT, etc., as well as interest on a bank loan. These figures
will take account of such things as payments due but not yet made
(but expected to be made) or payments made in advance. They will
also spread out major capital costs by including annual figures for
depreciation (how much value the purchased asset, in this case some

expensive kitchen equipment, has lost in a year), rather than the capital expenditure itself. These and other adjustments are intended to give both a true view of the profit or loss and one that is consistent from year to year, so that a comparison with previous years' accounts can safely be made. If the profit looks to be going up each year, then, generally speaking, it probably is. In this case, as the restaurant found its feet, it moved from an annual loss of £15,000 to an annual profit of £21,000. Note that while, in one sense, this is a major and very welcome change, the figures are still relatively modest when compared with the size of the business; performance is still very marginal. You need to keep everything in proportion.

One of the dangers of the adjustments that go into a Profit and Loss Account is that some problems might not show up, or not show up until far too late. Suppose, for example, that customers are continuing to buy your organization's products but getting slower and slower in paying for them, while the suppliers are pressing for faster and faster payment. This won't show up in the accounting profits, but it could be both a problem in itself and a sign of further problems ahead. The Cash Flow Statement gives an insight into this kind of issue by leaving out all the adjustments for pre- and post-payment, and just showing cash in and cash out. It also puts in the full purchase price of an asset, rather than the artificial figure for depreciation. But it includes all cash that comes in, including, for example, any money borrowed from the bank to make that purchase. In the case of the restaurant, there is not a massive differ-

	March 31, 2014	March 31, 2015
Fixed assets (lease, fixtures and fittings)	70,000	59,000
Stock	7,000	7,000
Cash	2,000	20,000
Trade creditors	(14,000)	(10,000)
Net assets	65,000	76,000
Bank loans	60,000	50,000
Issued share capital	10,000	10,000
Reserves	(5,000)	16,000
	65,000	76,000

Simple restaurant balance sheet

ence, but the improved profitability shows up in a greatly improved cash flow, even after repaying some of the bank loan.

Bank loans will also show up on the Balance Sheet. This lacks the intuitive simplicity of the other documents, but essentially shows the assets and liabilities of the enterprise, divided into categories. So the assets include a valuation for fixed assets, such as property and plant; other tangible assets ('things'); financial investments; cash in the bank; and money owed to the enterprise by outsiders, typically trade debtors (i.e. customers). On the liabilities' side are money owed by the enterprise to trade creditors (i.e. suppliers), to pension obligations, and to banks and other lenders, typically divided into short-term and long-term debts. What is left may come under a variety of headings (issued share capital, reserves, etc.) but is essentially the residual value of the enterprise: what would be left if everything was sold off and all accounts settled. In the case of the restaurant, there are no significant debtors but there are trade creditors – suppliers whose bills have not yet been sent or settled. And we again see the benefit of improved cash flow as the figure for creditors has declined, suggesting that bills are being paid more promptly. The issued share capital here is just what the owner put into the firm at start-up, and reserves are what are left when everything else has been accounted for.

We tend to think of accounting as if it were all black and white – it isn't. Even within the standard rules set by national and international accounting bodies, there are many ways of presenting financial accounts, depending on how things are valued and how they are classified. A trained accountant, looking at key financial ratios and probing the footnotes to work out exactly how a set of accounts has been put together, will be able not only to read far more from them than someone without that training, but also to spot areas of concern, where things might have been fudged to make them look better than they are. But anyone with basic numeracy skills and a bit of perseverance should be able to get a rough idea, most of the time, how viable an enterprise is, how that is changing over time and where the major risk areas lie.

Financial accounts are intended primarily for outside stakeholders. Management accounts are what an organization uses to analyse its operations for internal purposes, to control its costs and to forecast and budget for the future. In most organizations they are not widely shared and what you are most likely to see, as a manager, is a budget for your unit. This may include estimates for both income and expenditure. It may just take the form of allowable budgets for different categories of cost.

The first thing you will need to know in order to read or write a budget is what comes under each category of expense, which isn't always obvious, as the categories will be designed for accounting purposes, not for your purposes. So it's wise to ask. If the budget includes overhead costs, for office space, for example, or for centrally provided services, you will also want to find out how these are calculated. Are they based on your staff head-count, on wages and salaries, on square metres of space or on applying a multiplier to other costs? Or are they just picked out of the air by someone at the centre? You may not be able to do much about them, but sometimes you can. And even if you can't, understanding how they work will give you a valuable insight into the financial basis of the organization as a whole. Often the costs you see and can control are only a very small part of the total costs of operating a unit. The temptation is to complain that the overhead charges are far too high, but you cannot reasonably make this argument if you don't first understand how they come about.

As an illustration of a budget, consider Polly's budget for the primary school, as shown in the illustration. Since this a non-profit organization, income and expenditure are budgeted to cancel out. Income is set according to various formulae by the Local Education Authority, which also stipulates the premises' costs and puts vari-

Income	
Basic per pupil budget: 156 pupils @ £3015	470,340
High needs top-up	95,000
SEN and other allowances	50,500
	615,840
Budgeted expenditure	
Teaching staff salaries (incl. NI, pension, supply teachers, maternity cover etc.)	440,000
Other salaries	38,000
Premises costs (rates, overhead charge)	62,000
Equipment and teaching resources	12,500
IT	7,500
Utilities	6,000
Miscellaneous education costs	2,400
Cleaning and maintenance	43,000
Miscellaneous supplies and services	4,440
	615,840

Simple primary school budget

ous restrictions on other expenditures. By far the biggest cost in any state primary school, where the premises are, in effect, heavily subsidized, is the cost of salaries, and it's worth noting that these are much higher than the people receiving them might imagine. The school has to pay National Insurance charges and pension contributions on top of the employees' salary, and to allow for supply teaching when people are ill, on maternity leave or secondment and so on.

Organizations vary in how much latitude they give you over your budget: what areas of expenditure you are allowed to control; whether the budget is an estimate or a limit; how much freedom you have to spend more on one thing and less on another; whether allowances can be carried from one year to another; and so on. Depending on how much freedom you have, you may also have to decide how much freedom to give subsidiary budget-holders within your unit. And if you do give people freedom, you will need to think in advance about what you'll do if they overspend – or indeed if they underspend, perhaps through false economies. Your key resources here are basic numeracy, common sense and a sense of proportion, both in yourself and in any budget-holders for whom you are responsible.

Good managers should not be fretting about their spending and calculating it mechanistically. They should be sufficiently aware of their budgets and of how they're spending against them to make spending decisions without having to check the details. They should also be aware, critically, of how different kinds of expenditure contribute to the value added by their units, so that they can spend intelligently. It helps a lot if budget-holders are involved in writing their own budgets, in consultation with their managers, so that they know why the budgets have been drawn up as they have. And in writing a budget you – and they – should not just be doing the same as last year, but asking whether last year's allocations are still appropriate, given the objectives of the unit, and how they might be improved.

Not everyone has the abilities this requires and, while most people can be coached, you may have people reporting to you who either spend mechanically according to the figures you give them or consistently overspend. In such cases you have little option but to take control yourself, at least in the short term, use the budgets as control mechanisms and make sure they're adhered to.

The other area of financial management you should seek to understand is project finance. From time to time most organizations will make investments in the future. They will develop new products, invest in new facilities or new IT, engage consultants and so on. The basis of such investments is simple: you spend money in the short term to deliver returns, or improved returns, in the longer term. But when is an investment worthwhile?

In the simplest terms, if you invest, say £100,000 in some project, you will want to get returns of at least £100,000 more than if you hadn't made the investment; but it's not quite that simple. If you have to borrow the £100,000, then your returns will have to cover the borrowing costs as well, and even if you don't have to borrow it, you have to take account of what you would be able to do with the money if the project didn't happen – invest it in the financial markets, perhaps, or in another part of the organization. What this means is that your returns will generally have to be higher than your expenditure, and the further out they are in the future, the higher they will have to be. So what we do is apply a discount rate. If the discount rate is, say, 5 per cent, then £100,000 today is worth the same as £105,000 in a year's time, £110,250 in two years' time (applying the 5 per cent uplift twice in succession) and so on.

Now we can do a simple calculation. We can add up all the expected benefits from the project, use a discount rate to adjust them to an equivalent value today (so with a 5 per cent discount rate a benefit of £110,250 in two years' time would be equivalent to £100,000 today) and compare them with the costs of the project, similarly adjusted. Over more than a couple of years the calculation becomes too complicated to do in your head, but you can find net present value calculators online to do it for you. Note that most projects will involve some future costs, as well as initial ones, and that to do the calculation properly you need to estimate not only the total costs and benefits, but their detailed timings and the implications of this for cash flow.

The calculation will give you a first estimate of the viability of the project, but it entails two kinds of uncertainty. First, there will be some uncertainty both about the cost (project costs have a nasty habit of over-running) and especially about the returns. If you develop a new product to be introduced in three years, for example, you won't know in advance how much of it you will be able to sell at what price: you will have to make an informed guess and the evidence is that this is likely to be an over-optimistic one. Second, there will be uncertainty over the appropriate discount rate, with good arguments for any of a number of choices.

There are various ways of dealing with these uncertainties mathematically. If you don't have the appropriate technical training,

		Cash impact	NPV Discount rate = 6%	NPV Discount rate = 4%
Initial costs				
Lease premium (8 years on lease)	90,000			
Fitting out	125,000			
Launch and start-up costs	120,000			
	335,000	-335,000	-335,000	-335,000
Forecast annual profit				
Years 1-5	60,000	300,000	252,742	267,109
Years 6-8 (allowing for extra maintenance costs)	54,000	162,000	107,861	123,169
Impact on existing branches				
Years 1-3	-10,000	-30,000	-26,730	-27750
Years 4-8	5,000	25,000	17,682	19786
Total cash inflow		122,000		
Total NPV			16,555	47,314

Project valuation for new garage branch

however, the best approach, as in other matters involving planning and forecasting, is to try out a range of assumptions, both optimistic and pessimistic, and a range of discount rates, always keeping the calculations as simple as possible. (Too much detail is just a distraction.) In many cases, you will find that the answer falls out: on any reasonable assumptions the project will either work or not work. In other cases, the costing will be so tight and the projected returns so modest that the project is probably not worth thinking about. Sometimes you will be faced with real uncertainty, but you will at least have a basis for exploring where the problems lie, so that if you do go ahead, you will be alert to the risks.

A final thing to remember here is that while many investments are not really worth it, when you take a realistic view of the figures, not investing can also be a big risk, especially if it just delays the inevitable. So always do the calculations for non-investment as well as for investment, and accept that organizations do have to take risks if they are to survive and prosper. The trick is to take them knowingly.

For a simple, partial illustration, consider some of the calculations that George's company did when deciding recently whether to open a new branch of the dealership. They had been looking to expand the company and a good site had become available on an eight-year lease. Working out the estimated start-up costs and profitability of the branch over eight years gave the numbers in the figure above. As can be seen, in simple cash terms the investment looked very profitable, but once a discount rate was applied it became more marginal. Assuming a discount rate of 6 per cent, there was very little to be gained at all, and even at 4 per cent they would have to be very confident of their estimates, both of the new branch's profitability and of the impact on their existing branch network, which they thought would be negative to start with, as it took away customers, but positive later on through synergies and the extra service offered. They decided not to go ahead.

CHAPTER 5

Performance

Management accounts can give you an insight into your costs, but they don't generally tell you much about the other side of the operating equation – the value added. If your unit is a profit centre, you will have a simple monetary measure of that in the form of your revenues, whether from sales, donations (in a charity) or internal transfers. But knowing what your revenues are, and how they change from year to year, is one thing. Understanding what lies behind them, the value created for customers or donors, is another. Managing without this understanding is rather like managing without knowing how your costs break down: it's difficult to do things better, if you don't know what you're doing in the first place.

The most useful tool in this context is the value chain. There are several versions of this, but the most influential is that due to the Harvard Business School professor, Michael Porter. This is designed for the analysis of a large and complex business, but the basic idea can also be applied to a unit within a business, or indeed within any kind of organization.

The first thing to do is to divide up the unit being analysed into its constituent activities. If you're managing a manufacturing company, these might be line activities like purchasing, inbound logistics, manufacturing, marketing, sales, distribution and after-sales' service, together with support activities such as research and development, IT, accounts, human resources and so on. Most other enterprises, from a hotel to an accounting firm or an aid charity to a government agency, will be made up of similar sets of activities.

If your concern is with a functional unit within a larger organization, you will break the activities down further. So, if you're managing a call centre, for example, the line activities might include recruitment, training, call handling, customer interface, etc., while some of the core activities of the business you're serving (manufacturing, for example, or after-sales service) might for you be support activities.

The value chain concept contains two basic ideas. The first is that, however you divide up the activities, each adds some value to the end customer (or, if it doesn't, you shouldn't be doing it). The second is that value can also be added (or not) by the relationships between activities – in particular, by the ways in which information and understanding are shared across the organization, and the operations of one part are attuned to the needs of another.

To conduct a simple value chain analysis, draw a circle for each activity, including those that link your unit to other units or to customers and suppliers, and draw connecting lines whenever one activity depends on another. You might use different coloured lines for physical transfers, information transfers and shared background information. Then ask what value is added by each activity and across each link, how and where this could be enhanced, and how cost-effective each element of value adding is or could be. The answers won't always be obvious. The working of the links, in particular, can sometimes be quite subtle. But if you persevere by asking questions and, of course, by asking questions of the people involved, you should significantly enhance your understanding of the unit and how it can be managed to deliver more than it is at present.

By way of illustrations, consider the value chains for Rick's restaurant business and the maternity unit of the hospital where Melanie is matron. In the restaurant, the value added is clearly measured by how much the customers, in aggregate, pay for their meals. The profit of the enterprise is the difference between this and the total costs incurred. Value is added most obviously by the

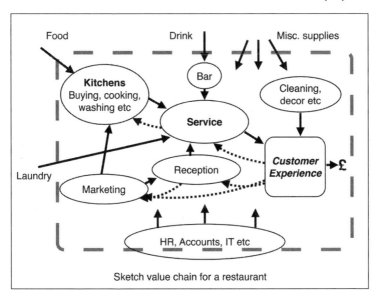

Sketch value chain for a restaurant

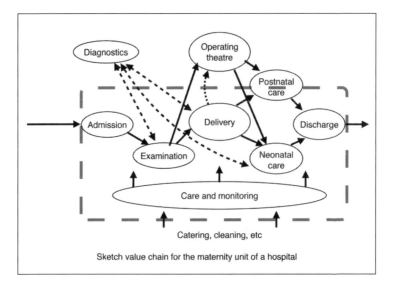

Sketch value chain for the maternity unit of a hospital

activities that impinge directly on customers – the activities of the kitchens, above all, and of the front-of-house staff. But it is also added by the creation and maintenance of a physical environment, by a range of supporting activities and by the synergies between activities: by the feedback loops between the front-of-house staff observing the customer experience, the kitchens and the marketing activities, for example.

In the case of the hospital, the value added is much harder to measure: it lies in positive birthing experiences, healthy mothers and children, and so on. The activities are also harder to pin down, as they form part of a much larger and more complex organization, through which patients might take multiple routes. But we can still sketch out roughly the main activities concerned and how they impinge on outcomes, and this gives us a picture both of how the unit adds value and of how other units in the hospital contribute to that. As in the case of the restaurant, value is added by the way the system processes information – particularly, in this case, medical information, but also information on the patient's concerns and worries – to where it is needed, as well as by the way it processes people and things.

Another useful approach to the assessment of performance or value added is through the use of key performance indicators (KPIs). The idea here is that in any unit there will be a number of outcomes you can measure, each of which will give an insight into some aspect of performance. A simple example would be in a restaurant, where two key indicators are the number of people served each day (absolutely or as a proportion of the maximum capacity) and the spend per person. Because a restaurant has relatively high fixed costs, which are the same no matter how many customers there are, it matters a lot how full you are. (Air travel and hotels are similar.) And because the prices of dishes and drinks are much higher than the cost of the food or drink, it matters a lot how much people spend. A successful restaurant is one that is always crowded, and where people are tempted, once in, to spend a lot. A third indicator might be the amount of repeat business. If you want to build a sustainable business, you will want customers to return and to recommend the place to their friends,

None of these indicators tells the whole story. There may well be a trade-off between the number of people you can get in and the amount they spend, for example, and there are other considerations too – the amount of food wasted, staff turnover and so on. But you will do a much better job of managing the restaurant if you have a close eye on the indicators, than if you just look at the total takings. In particular, each one points towards specific things that can be done to improve performance.

Although there are some generic KPIs (financial ratios, for example, or customer satisfaction ratings), the most useful ones tend to be quite specific to the business, function or activity concerned. Indeed, part of their value lies in the very process of working out

Key performance indicator	Possible benchmarks
SATS results, year 6	National averages for schools with similar catchments. Best performing local school.
SATS results, improvement from year 2 to year 6	National averages for schools with similar catchments. Best performing local school.
OFSTED assessments	Outstanding
Proportion playing a musical instrument	
Sports participation levels	
Teacher turnover	Local education authority top quartile
Teacher sickness	Local education authority top quartile
Pupil attendance	Local education authority top quartile
Admission applications from locality	

Some key performance indicators for a primary school

what they should be. You think about the things you might measure and ask, in each case, what does this tell us and what does it not tell us. Sometimes the indicators you use will be quite standard for the sector or function you're in, but sometimes you might light upon something quite quirky that just happens to work for your unit.

As a simple illustration, consider the KPIs adopted by Polly for her primary school. Some of these are set for her, like the pupil test results. But Polly is interested in more than just test results. She is interested, for example, in the overall growth and development of her children, and finds that music and sports participation are useful measures of this. Teacher turnover and absence rates give her indicators of the classroom environment, and so do attendance rates. At primary level, truancy is not a problem, but when children are off sick a lot, that can be an indicator of unhappiness at school or problems at home. She is also interested in where local people prefer to send their children: if it is not to their most local school, that suggests a problem.

Where you adopt a standard KPI, it may sometimes be possible to benchmark performance against similar units or organizations. Arts charities, for example, tend to have sponsorship categories associated with different levels of donation, and publicize the number of donations at each level; so, if that's your business, you can compare yourselves directly with others. Published accounts of businesses include a variety of measures that can be used to construct indicators, and others can be constructed from market research reports or analyses in the trade press. In Polly's case, some data are collected nationally and some by the Local Education Authority.

The main purpose of benchmarking is to compare your unit with best practice elsewhere. So you will normally be looking to benchmark wherever possible against an exemplary unit or organization, ideally one that works under similar conditions or constraints to your own, and to learn from whatever they do better than you. A very common practice is to benchmark against the average but, while this has its uses, it is essentially defensive and always looks that way to outsiders. Moreover, an average organization doesn't actually exist, so there is nothing you can learn from it. It may be useful to know what you do better or worse than the average, but the important thing is to know how you can improve, and that improvement might come just as well from making something that was already average excellent, as from making something that was poor average.

A final point, that should perhaps be obvious but is easily overlooked, is that the choice of KPIs should ideally be based on a thoughtful cost and value chain analysis, and performance against benchmarks should be analysed in this light. So, going back to Rick's restaurant, for example, the chef might cook the most wonderful meals but he has to do so to a budget, and the KPIs need to reflect this. Similarly, while customer satisfaction surveys might provide one indicator, this needs to be reflected in repeat business and referrals. Each of the three techniques – value chain analysis, KPIs and benchmarking – is much more powerful when used in conjunction with the others than when used in isolation.

PERFORMANCE AND MOTIVATION

One of the uses to which KPIs are sometimes put is to analyse the performance of an individual or team. The indicators are used to set performance targets, and the achievement or non-achievement of those targets is used in performance appraisal, promotion decisions and performance-related pay.

This raises a number of problems. Of course, it makes perfect sense, in most contexts, to identify performance targets, to monitor people's performance against those targets and to reward good performance, whether directly through the pay packet or indirectly through promotion through the ranks of an organization. But you have to be careful, first, not to damage people's self-motivation; and, second, not to motivate them to meet artificial targets at the expense of the much more complex, all-round performance that will most benefit the organization. And you have to be very careful in conducting performance appraisals that you don't do more harm than good.

Performance appraisal is a key part of any manager's job and a very valuable tool, yet most organizations give little, or indeed any, training in it. There may be a form to fill in and instructions as to who should fill in what and when. There may be nothing at all. Many managers treat it as an administrative chore to be got through as quickly as possible. (I once met my appraiser in the corridor. 'How are you John?' 'Very well, thanks.' 'Good, I'll send over the forms for your signature.') Where there is no direct link to pay or promotion, many appraisees see it as a waste of time, and where there is a link, there is often mistrust of the process.

If you are introducing a new performance appraisal system, you will need to read about how to do it at far greater length than is possible here. The task with which managers are usually faced, however, is making an existing system work. What you need to know then is how appraisal systems are supposed to work, in general terms, and something about the practices that help or hinder that.

Performance appraisal is conventionally divided into four phases: planning, execution, assessment and review. Each is important. The planning phase involves agreeing with appraisees and writing down, each year: their key job responsibilities; the key skills and competencies required to execute these; a set of goals or targets; and an individual development plan, including both training, where appropriate, and self-development.

The job responsibilities (what is to be done) and competencies (how it is to be done) are sometimes omitted from the process but should be a critical part of it, since they provide the context for everything else. They should be both more and less than those specified in a job description. More, in the sense of adding flesh to the bare bones, filling out what is required. And less, in the sense of focusing on a relatively few factors: those that are key to the job and those that might usefully be developed. The skills and competencies here may be job-specific, but they may also be general (interpersonal skills, for example) or organization-specific (skills that will be valued across the organization).

At the heart of the appraisal process are the general goals and more specific, often quantitative, performance targets on which the appraisee will be assessed. Some of the targets might be formally imposed as criteria for promotion or as part of a performance-related pay package. Others may be based on your own analysis of the responsibilities and competencies that have been identified, and on any key performance indicators you have identified for the unit.

The important thing here is to see the goals and targets as a package, to make sure that that package fits together in a meaningful way and to make sure that it works in motivational terms. The goals and targets need to make sense not only in terms of the responsibilities and competencies of the job, but also, more broadly, in terms of the goals and strategy of the unit and of the organization as a whole. They need ideally to be consistent with each other and, where there are tensions (for example, between a specific performance target and a more general goal, only part of which it captures), you need to discuss these explicitly with appraisees, so that they don't act as a silent cloud of doubt and confusion, producing conflicting and self-cancelling motivations.

As we have already discussed, performance targets should normally be stretching and challenging, but not unrealistically beyond reach. It is the challenge of a job that is generally the most important motivator for the person doing it, and there is no challenge in doing something easy or in being set something impossible. The appropriate degree of stretch, however, will vary from individual to individual. There is no one size fits all. Finally, you should take special care that the extrinsic motivation of money doesn't crowd out the intrinsic motivations of rising to a challenge, helping and working with others, and doing a good job. You can't expect people to ignore or downplay the money – if achieving a certain target earns them extra pay, they will quite reasonably want to achieve that target and to have your support in doing so. But you can make sure that the non-monetary goals and targets are emphasized too, and assure an appraisee that achievements there will be recognized and appreciated.

The execution phase of performance appraisal is often omitted, but is again vital. It is no good just setting someone targets and going back a year later to see whether they have been achieved. You also need to be monitoring progress, providing feedback and coaching, so as to help the person achieve those targets, as well as providing encouragement and recognition, especially of those things that are not formally recognized through the incentive and reward system of the organization. Sometimes you may need to remind them of the responsibilities, competencies, KPIs and goals you discussed at the beginning of the process. Wherever possible, though, this should be done in a positive and constructive way. As we have already noted, criticism rarely motivates.

Towards the end of the cycle you will have to prepare a written assessment of both the appraisee's performance and their development over the year (the appraisee will have to do likewise), and use that as a basis to conduct a face-to-face review. This in turn will lead into the preparation for the coming year's planning meeting.

Where people are performing well, the assessment and review should be straightforward. The appraisees will be looking to stretch themselves further; you will be congratulating them on their progress and working with them towards future goals. Where people are not performing well, however, you will have to strike a careful balance. On one hand, you won't want to demotivate them by being too critical. On the other hand, you won't want to fudge things by avoiding criticism. Here you need to separate facts from attitudes. Your attitude should be supportive, encouraging and sympathetic. Helping people to do their jobs better is, after all, the crux of your job. But the facts of any performance shortfall should be told straight, and the discussion of how to improve things should be frank and open. So if, for example, they have underperformed but have an excuse – emotional disturbances at home, for example – the latter is no reason to ignore the former. Both need to be addressed explicitly.

CHAPTER 6

Planning

One of the things we have emphasized in this book is the importance of planning. Another is that plans once made don't execute themselves. Implementation will always run up against obstacles of one kind or another, and needs careful monitoring and management, which must itself be planned. But how do you go about planning? The details vary, of course, depending on what is being planned, but crudely speaking there are two sides to planning. One is forecasting what will or may happen in the future. The other is deciding what you intend to happen in the future and putting it into practice.

Sometimes the purpose of the planning will be to anticipate future changes, so you will start with the forecasting and then work out how to respond to what that tells you. Sometimes the purpose will be to achieve a specific end, in which case the forecasting will be concerned with identifying risks and contingencies that might upset the plans. In both cases, however, there is an ongoing interaction between the two activities. You plan activities on the basis of your best knowledge or forecasts of the future, but make allowance for the uncertainty in this knowledge. Then, as you execute the plans, you adapt both the forecasts and the schedules in the light of the experience gained.

Various techniques can help you with this. On the forecasting side, there are techniques of financial planning and scenario planning. On the implementation side, there are techniques of project planning and scheduling. Risk management techniques are usually treated as part of the implementation side, but they are closely related to forecasting and effectively bridge the two sides.

Both financial planning and scenario planning address the problem of how to plan for the future in an uncertain world, where nothing can be predicted with confidence. Financial planning, in which the future is modelled on a spreadsheet, attempts to reduce the uncertainties to financial numbers (quantitative expectations and probabilities) and is used in situations where this can be more or less achieved. Scenario planning is concerned primarily with futures that are just too uncertain to be reliably quantified.

In financial planning, you are usually concerned with medium-term futures and with a relatively limited range of uncertainties that can effectively be reduced to numbers: to a set of financial projections and variations on those projections. You are essentially taking a set of management accounts and projecting them forward five or ten years, taking account of any information you have: of existing and planned projects, new or replacement assets, expected price changes, expected changes in customer demands and so on. The purpose is to keep control of the finances of the organization: to identify and plan for future funding needs and cash flow gaps, or cutbacks in expenditure, or alternatively to identify future surpluses and plan for their reinvestment.

Some of the figures in a financial plan will be fairly predictable. Some financial commitments, for example, may be fixed years in advance. And, in many organizations, some estimates of both costs and revenues should be reasonably robust, at least for the first couple of years of the plan. Even in the short term, however, things can happen to throw out your estimates, and the further forward you look, the more uncertain these estimates will be. A key part of financial planning is to take account of this uncertainty by testing the plan against different assumptions as to how things will go.

The simplest approach is to start with projections based on your best estimates, giving a 'base case'. You then ask what unknown factors might significantly affect the outcomes. You will not normally be interested in changes that will have only a marginal effect or in those that are extremely unlikely, but in those that have a reasonable chance of occurring and would have a significant impact. Depending on the organization and its circumstances, you might be looking, for example, at changes in interest rates or exchange rates (both notoriously difficult to predict), changes in customer demand or grant funding, or changes in the costs of energy or other key supplies. You then conduct a sensitivity analysis. You put these factors as variables into your financial planning spreadsheet and see what happens to the end result (the profitability and cash flow of the organization, its funding needs and so on) when they are varied up or down.

Your main concern in financial planning will typically be with the downside, so you will look to come up with three or four versions of the plan: one showing your best estimate and the others showing its sensitivity to various not improbable circumstances – interest rates up 3 per cent and demand down 5 per cent, say, or whatever seems appropriate. The figures you use are a matter of judgement and are best chosen through discussion. As with the factors you choose to focus on, you will normally want to stay within the bounds of reasonable possibilities, but you will also want to be open to such possibilities and not to be complacent in any way. And one of the main points of the different variants of the plan is to encourage discussion. How confident are you of your projections? How likely are the different projected outcomes? Should you change your base plan assumptions, either now or in the next planning cycle? What contingency plans should you draw up in case things should turn out badly? What precautionary measures should you take now? What indicators do you need to monitor most closely?

As an example, let's take Ed's engineering company. Each year Ed is required to report to the chief executive and finance director of the parent company with a ten-year financial plan for his subsidiary. To create this he starts out with the current performance and extrapolates that to take account of the known elements of company strategy, likely environmental changes and so on. The figures are in constant prices, i.e. ignoring inflation, which is accounted for only when it affects some things more than others.

This plan assumes steady growth outside the UK, based on growth of sales in process instrumentation (instrumentation of automated process in factories) and specialist instrumentation for ships and aeroplanes, with costs generally growing not quite as fast as revenues. But as we've noted repeatedly, plans don't always work out, and alongside the base plan Ed presents the impacts of different

£ million	2015	2016	2017	2018	2019	2020	2021	2022	2023	2024
Sales	25.0	25.5	26.0	26.5	27.0	27.5	28.0	28.5	29.0	29.5
By region										
UK	8.0	8.0	8.0	8.0	8.0	8.0	8.0	8.0	8.0	8.0
Rest of Europe	13.0	13.3	13.6	13.9	14.2	14.5	14.8	15.1	15.4	15.7
Rest of World	4.0	4.2	4.4	4.6	4.8	5.0	5.2	5.4	5.6	5.8
By division										
Process instrumentation	14.0	14.4	14.8	15.2	15.6	16.0	16.4	16.8	17.2	17.6
Ship / Aero instrumentation	6.0	6.3	6.6	6.9	7.2	7.5	7.8	8.1	8.4	8.7
General engineering	5.0	4.8	4.6	4.4	4.2	4.0	3.8	3.6	3.4	3.2
Cost of manufacturing	16.0	16.3	16.6	16.9	17.2	17.5	17.8	18.1	18.4	18.7
Sales and marketing	1.8	2.0	2.0	2.0	2.0	2.0	2.0	2.0	2.0	2.0
Research and development	1.0	1.0	1.0	1.0	1.0	1.0	1.0	1.0	1.0	1.0
Administration and overheads	2.6	2.6	2.6	2.7	2.7	2.7	2.8	2.8	2.8	2.9
Central overheads	1.4	1.4	1.4	1.4	1.4	1.4	1.4	1.4	1.4	1.4
Profit	2.2	2.2	2.4	2.5	2.7	2.9	3.0	3.2	3.4	3.5

Simplified financial base plan for an engineering business

£ million	2015	2016	2017	2018	2019	2020	2021	2022	2023	2024
Base plan sales	25.0	25.5	26.0	26.5	27.0	27.5	28.0	28.5	29.0	29.5
Base plan profits	2.2	2.2	2.4	2.5	2.7	2.9	3.0	3.2	3.4	3.5
Variation A:										
Sales	25.0	25.5	26.0	27.0	28.0	30.0	31.0	32.0	33.0	33.5
Profits	2.2	2.2	2.4	2.6	2.8	3.1	3.2	3.3	3.4	3.5
Variation B:										
Sales	25.0	25.5	26.0	26.0	25.0	23.0	22.0	22.0	22.0	22.0
Profits	2.2	2.2	2.4	2.2	2.0	1.2	1.0	1.2	1.2	1.2

Variation A: Global economic boom, partially offset by deteriorating value of pound and increased Chinese competition, resulting in increased turnover but reduced margins.

Variation B: Global economic recession, pound holds value, some disruption to Eastern Europe markets, resulting in some loss of both turnover and margins.

Engineering business financial plan: summary sensitivity analysis

contingencies. Global recession would impact badly on the business generally, but especially the ship and aeroplane sides, while a global boom would be good for business. Since the costs are all incurred in the UK, and most of the revenues are overseas, changes in the relative value of the pound to other currencies could have a big effect. The growth of the Chinese economy is also a factor, as Ed is expecting, at some point, to face serious competition from Chinese firms. Finally, some of the company's biggest markets for process engineering are in Eastern European countries with high political risks. For financial planning purposes, Ed looks at the possible impacts of all these factors on the company over the next ten years and conducts some sensitivity analyses. The document he presents includes a range of spreadsheets and much more detail than can be shown here, but the headline figures look something like the illustration above.

Ed's financial planning is based at root on a business-as-usual model. The environment may change but the company will adapt, and so will its competitors. He is well aware, however, that some of the possibilities he has envisaged may mean that business is very much not as usual. Given the strategy of the parent company, Eagle Engineering is unlikely to become a hotbed of innovation and achieve rapid growth, but it could be seriously threatened. While he can envisage such a possibility, however, he cannot really visualize it and he cannot put meaningful numbers on it. Another kind of planning is needed.

Scenario planning was developed by the oil giant Shell as a tool for planning in the very long term, twenty to thirty years, and in the context of major political, economic and technological uncertainties. The basic technique is, however, useful in a much wider range of conditions, both for systematically analysing future uncertainties and much more generally for helping people to think outside the box.

The idea behind scenario planning is that we live in a very uncertain world, which cannot be reduced to quantitative trends and variations on them – a world in which we cannot even put a probability on key possibilities and in which the range of such possibilities is too wide to be captured in a spreadsheet. In such an uncertain world we cannot hope to make meaningful forecasts, but we can try to capture a wide range of possible futures and so prepare ourselves for whatever might arise.

The first step in a scenario planning exercise is similar to the identification of key factors in a financial planning exercise, but more wide-reaching. You try to think of all the things that could happen over the next twenty or thirty years that might impact significantly on your organization. This is a blue skies' exercise and you want to be as open as possible in your thinking, so it helps to work with a group of (preferably) imaginative colleagues. You might be looking at environmental, political, technological, social or economic changes and, in particular, at areas of great uncertainty. In a typical exercise today, the focus is likely to be on things like climate change, population demographics, breakthroughs in areas like robotics or genetics, major economic recessions, and changes in the balance of global economic and political power. But you should also be thinking of things more specific to your industry or organization – anything that could impact significantly on the environment in which you operate.

Having come up with as many factors as you can, you classify them, very roughly, in terms of low, medium and high likelihood (you won't be able to assign any quantitative probabilities, but that doesn't matter), and low, medium and high impact on the organization and what it does. Next, focus on the factors in the high-likelihood/high-impact category, and if that's empty, or nearly so, on those in the medium-high and high-medium categories. Using combinations of these, construct three highly speculative but plausible scenarios or possible futures. Between them, you want these scenarios to cover a wide range of possibilities, so they will likely be very different from each other. Next fill out these three pictures so that your scenarios become future worlds rich enough for you to think yourself into them, and ask what the implications of each would be for your organization. How much would you have to change the way you operate and in what ways? Are there developments you should be looking at now to prepare yourself better to face these futures?

Thinking through some of the high-impact and high-likelihood factors that might impact on Eagle Engineering, Ed has identified several that seem worthy of consideration. Global warming and widespread water shortages already look very likely, and these could have a significant impact on the strength and stability of different economies. The increasing power of China and the growing tensions between Russia and the West could impact massively on world trade and the terms of trade, disrupting Eagle's markets. It was also easy to see a situation with the growth of Chinese and East Asian engineering in which a UK-based engineering company would simply not be viable, competitively. The growth of digital automation also raised the possibility of a world in which conventional instrumentation – purpose-built instruments designed to be read by humans – would be redundant. But how to take account of these? Ed has set four teams, drawn from his young staff, the task of portraying how the world might look in 2040. He doesn't know what they might come up with, but that's the point.

While scenario planning was designed to address long-term futures, the basic mix of unfettered blue skies thinking, sorting potentially relevant factors according to their likelihood and impact, and generating plausible scenarios from combinations of these, has a much wider applicability. It can be used, for example, as part of financial planning or as part of project planning. In both cases it helps you to avoid getting stuck within a particular mindset based on your own personal way of looking at things and the prevailing assumptions of the moment. It helps you to combine creative, imaginative thinking with focused, relevant analysis.

Again, while the techniques were developed for large corporations, they can be applied to any organization. George's car dealership, for example, might build scenarios around future planning regimes, the possibility of internet sales direct from the manufacturer, the reduced servicing requirements as car technology develops and changes in the way people finance large purchases. It will be some time before Rick dares to think of long-term futures for his restaurant, but his neighbour on the high street, a long-established family clothes shop that owns its own premises, needs to be thinking now about what the high street might look like in ten or fifteen years' time, and how people might then be shopping for clothes.

PROJECT PLANNING AND SCHEDULING

The type of planning you are most likely to be engaged in as a manager is project planning. Projects come in all shapes and sizes. You may be constructing a new building, installing new machinery, changing IT systems or launching a new product. You may be changing the way your services are delivered, moving offices or just moving the office around. Whatever the project, however, it will go through much the same stages, beginning with an idea, progressing through approval of a set of objectives and, where appropriate, a financial case, to detailed planning of the work, implementation and final delivery. We don't have space here to cover the whole process, so we shall focus on a few key points and the techniques associated with them.

The first requirement of any project is a precisely specified set of deliverables, chosen to meet a set of objectives within a set of constraints. There is no particular technique needed here, just clarity and rigour. The objectives must be clear and they must be rooted in the strategy and objectives of the organization and unit. A commonly used criterion is that they should be SMART: Strategic, Measurable, Agreed, Realistic and Timed. The constraints will typically be constraints of time, money and human resources, and need to be rigorously applied. There is no point setting out on a project and discovering half-way through that it doesn't meet the organization's objectives or cannot be completed due to a lack of money or resources.

One of the things you will need to do in order to specify your deliverables is to make estimates of time and cost for each component activity. Only by doing that will you be able to judge whether what you're specifying will in fact be deliverable within the project constraints. Estimating is not easy. We are always reading of major projects that have gone way over the initial budget and/or timescale. But there are some simple techniques that can help a lot.

The most reliable way to estimate time and cost is by comparison with a very similar project, but if you can't do this you will have to work things out from scratch. Begin with a first draft of the project deliverables: what you would like to be able to deliver and what you think, on the basis of experience, that you should be able to deliver within the constraints operating. Then work backwards and set down everything that will have to be done in order to get to these deliverables. Break it down first into a number of stages, each with its own deliverables, then break these stages down into sub-stages and so on until you get down to a set of tasks, each of which is well enough defined for you to be able to estimate, fairly confidently,

Task	Work units
Stripping out, clearing, cleaning, carrying etc.	Labourers: 30 days
Re-partitioning	Carpenters: 6 days Labourers: 3 days
Replace/repair doors, windows etc	Joiners: 20 days
First fix plumbing and electrics	Plumbers: 4 days Electricians: 4 days Carpenters: 2 days
Plastering and screeding	Plasterers: 6 days
Bathrooms installation	Plumbers: 4 days carpenters: 2 days
Kitchen installation	Plumbers: 1 day Joiners: 6 days
Second fix electrics and testing	Electricians: 2 days
Tiling and decorating	Tilers: 6 days Decorators: 12 days

Work breakdown for a domestic building project: alterations and renovations

the work needed. Conventional wisdom is that you should work with units no larger than a person-week, but this will depend on the tasks themselves, and your knowledge and experience of them.

When Growlers, the car dealership, was considering setting up a new branch, the costs we summarized in an earlier example were ultimately based on a work breakdown structure. The project was split into a number of (overlapping) phases, for example: acquisition; design, planning and permissions; fitting out; staff recruitment and training; workshop stocking; trade stocking (new cars, demonstrators, used cars); and launch activities. Each of these was a significant project in itself, so had to be further sub-divided and only then could a breakdown be made into work units.

For a more straightforward project, consider one of Brad the builder's contracts, for alterations and renovations to a large house. In this kind of situation, Brad may draw up a specification of works himself, having talked to the client, or he may tender a price on the basis of a contract specification provided by an architect or surveyor. Either way the client's specification, in terms of the finished product, has to be converted into a specification in terms of the work to be done, which can then be costed. The illustration above shows how Brad might go about costing and estimating the direct labour for a project in which he's working directly with the client.

Having broken down the work needed for a project, you can begin to estimate costs. For small projects, work out the gross salary cost (don't forget employer contributions) of each task, assuming around 180 working days a year (after sickness, training, etc.). For larger projects, estimate an average cost per task and just multiply up. Then multiply up again to allow for overheads. A large organization will usually have a standard multiplier for overhead costs but in a smaller organization you may need to look historically at how your costs are made up. Overheads have to cover all the administration and support, machinery and premises and their maintenance, fuel and utility costs and more, and they always come to more than you'd think. They typically double or triple the salary cost. Add in your best estimates for materials, consultancy, professional services and so on. And when you have a figure for the total project, double it – yes, double it, or at least double that part of it that is not made up of fixed cost supplies. With the best will in the world we always underestimate costs, so in working out the feasibility of a project by estimating costs from scratch, a good rule of thumb is just to double the number you first get to. If you are working from a close comparison or from a lot of relevant experience, you will be able to make a smaller adjustment, but even if you're absolutely confident of your estimates, you will still need to add 20 per cent and, in most cases, you will need to add much, much more.

These adjustments to your raw calculations will feature in your project planning as contingency costs. In a complex project you will generally have higher contingencies than in a simple one, and you will spread them across the project stages, with the bulk being set against the stages that are further down the line and so less certain. On completion of each stage, you will recalculate the contingency for the rest of the project and reallocate it to the remaining stages, hoping always that as the project progresses, certainty will increase and the percentage contingency can be reduced. If you find yourself using up your contingency quickly, however, alarm bells should ring: your original allowance might not be enough and the feasibility of the project might be called into question. At this point you have to face the music. Never, ever, just hope that things will improve!

Estimates and contingencies for time are worked out in the same ways as those for cost, but in this case there is an added complication, in that the later stages of the project may not be able to start until the earlier ones are finished. So, as well as a work breakdown structure you will also need a project schedule. The most common tool for this is a simple Gantt chart, which is essentially a calendar along the top (a day or a week per column) with each task blocked in on a separate row. Three criteria apply in entering the

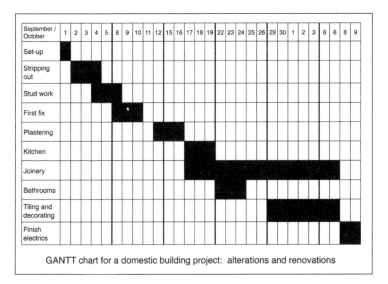

September / October	1	2	3	4	5	8	9	10	11	12	15	16	17	18	19	22	23	24	25	26	29	30	1	2	3	6	6	8	9
Set-up																													
Stripping out																													
Stud work																													
First fix																													
Plastering																													
Kitchen																													
Joinery																													
Bathrooms																													
Tiling and decorating																													
Finish electrics																													

GANTT chart for a domestic building project: alterations and renovations

tasks. First, nothing can be started until everything that needs to be finished first is finished first. Second, the timing of the tasks has to match the availability of the necessary people and other resources. In particular, if one person or team is responsible for two or more tasks on different projects, they will have to fit into separate time windows. Third, you will again have to allow for contingencies. These will generally be of the same order as the cost contingencies, and will be distributed across the stages and revised on completion of each stage in the same way.

The illustration shows an initial Gantt chart for Brad's building project, which he hopes to complete in six weeks. The problem for Brad, or rather for his client, is that this takes no account of other ongoing projects on which his various trades will be needed, so he really needs a giant Gantt chart covering all the projects in hand and making allowance both for the fact that a joiner cannot be working on two sites at once and for the impact of possible delays due to sickness, bad weather and so on. In practice he needs to time the beginning of each new project to fit in with the timings of progress on the others, and also to build in a contingency of about 20 per cent – in this case just over a week – of slack time.

As we discussed earlier in the book, any project runs a risk of running up against unexpected problems, both in terms of the project tasks themselves and in terms of events that might push everything off course. Contingency planning is one way of allowing for these risks, but it is a very passive way, just providing a time and cost buffer. For many projects you will also need to use some risk evaluation and risk management techniques. These same techniques can also be applied to the management of risk more generally.

Risk evaluation works in much the same way as scenario planning, but with the focus on a much shorter time period and on much more specific, locally impacting factors. It still helps to have some creative thinking, as the most dangerous risks are often those that no-one thinks of. And it is again helpful to categorize risks as low, medium or high likelihood and low, medium or high impact. Whereas scenario planning is about identifying a limited number of key factors, risk management is about not leaving out anything that might be significant, so you will not want to restrict yourself to the high/high, high/medium and medium/high categories of risk. But you will still need to prioritize these. Having identified and prioritized the significant risk factors, you then need to decide what to do about them. In some cases it may be that you can do something to prevent them or reduce their likelihood or impact. In some cases there may be nothing at all you can do except hope that they don't happen. In many cases, though, you will need to have in place some sort of contingency plan. If you have decided in advance what to do when a risk occurs, then you can make allowance for that within your cost and time contingencies. But if you haven't, then working out your response may in itself use up your time contingency and more, and as tasks have to be delayed, altered or rescheduled that will also add cost.

All the managers we have been following in this book have to undertake some kind of risk management. For Polly and Melanie, the main concerns are health and safety, rather than financial risks. They both maintain and regularly review risk registers. These list the risks that have been identified, together with the measures adopted to prevent or counter them, and contingency plans to mitigate their effects should they arise. George's firm hasn't yet got around to risk registers, but he is beginning to put one together for his own peace of mind. Ed's much larger firm is very risk-conscious, but with strict health and safety policies operating throughout the corporation, his own main focus is on financial risk. Heavily engaged in the local community, he also finds himself conducting more general risk analyses for the town festival and other events.

Belle's environment is so routinized that she doesn't have to think very much herself about the risks facing her organization but, like every manager in the bank, she is trained to beware of bad loans and anyone coming to her for a business loan has to present a risk analysis as part of their business plan. Brad's business is effectively

Risk	Likelihood	Impact	Preventative measures	Responses
Failed hygiene inspection	Low	High	Strict hygiene	Damage limitation through marketing / PR
Customer food poisoning	Low	Medium	Strict hygiene	Ditto
Fire	Low	High	Strict kitchen rules, regular fire drills	Rapid rebuild, retain key staff
Slated in review	Medium	Medium	Maintain high standards every day	Marketing / PR
Chef leaving	Medium	High	Attentive management, well-trained sous-chef	Keep file of possible candidates; replace fast
Maître d' leaving	Medium	Low	Attentive management	Replace fast
Change in fashion	Medium	Medium	None	Monitor carefully. be prepared to change formula
New competition	High	Medium	None	Marketing / PR
Proposed major building works next door	Medium	High	None	Retain core customers; consider relocation
Suspension of parking due to major road improvements	High	Medium	None	Retain core customers; temporarily downsize?

Schedule of some of the risks facing a restaurant

a succession of projects, each of which carries significant risks of various kinds: cost miscalculations, poor workmanship, major mistakes, site accidents, disagreements with the client, unpaid bills, the loss of key employees, bad weather and so on. Rick's restaurant, on the other hand, is just one ongoing project, which sometimes seems to be nothing but risk.

The illustration shows a rough schedule of the most significant risks to Rick's restaurant at the moment. Most of these are ongoing, but some arise from particular circumstances, so the register needs to be constantly reviewed and kept up to date.

CHAPTER 7

People

Since managing is essentially about managing people, it obviously helps if you can understand people: how they think, what motivates them, how they behave. And there are indeed many theories and frameworks you can draw on to help with this. In particular, there are numerous theories of motivation, and there are various techniques for analysing and classifying people's psychologies and personalities.

Unfortunately, these are generally less helpful than they appear. Theories of motivation tend to be just that: theories. It is certainly helpful to have in mind the range of factors that might motivate people, or might be used to motivate them: individual achievement, collective achievement, job satisfaction, personal growth or fulfilment, money, status, recognition. It is also helpful to have in mind the factors that might need to be in place before you can motivate them, even if they are not themselves motivators: some degree of job security, perhaps, an absence of conflict, recognition or approval, and money again. And it is helpful to be able to distinguish between the two, as some of the theories do. But there are no general rules of motivation.

Everybody is different. Money, for example, might be a positive motivator for one person, a basic requirement for another and more or less irrelevant for a third. One person will be motivated more by individual achievement, another by collective achievement and another only by achievements, of whatever kind, that are recognized and rewarded in some way. So your task as a manager is always to think about what motivates Louis or Louise, and for that the theories provide no more than checklists of possibilities.

Psychological profiling is used by many larger organizations, both in the appointments process and sometimes also in promotions decisions; for example, when appointing to a leadership position. But again there is a need for caution. If a test profiles for leadership traits, for example, the effect is to identify (and that only cautiously – these tests are not very discriminating) traits that have either been associated theoretically with leadership effectiveness or been associated empirically with perceived leadership effectiveness. But then perceived leadership effectiveness was most probably defined in the first place in terms of the traits being measured. So an analysis might tell you something about how someone responds to a questionnaire and it might raise topics for discussion, but it won't tell you whether someone will make a good leader. Both people and leadership are far too complex for that.

The other kind of psychological profiling in common use is typified by the Myers Briggs test, which is based on C. G. Jung's theory of psychological types. Jung identified three dimensions on which people's psychologies might vary: introverted (rooted in the internal world of one's own thoughts and ideas) versus extraverted (rooted in the external world of action and of other people's judgements); sensing versus intuition as ways of perceiving; and thinking versus feeling as ways of judging. Myers and Briggs added, as a fourth dimension, a person's preferences between perceiving and judging, making a four-dimensional typology.

As an insight into one's own psychology a Myers Briggs analysis is fascinating, but as a management tool it's not much use. It might tell you something about what's likely to influence people and how they might respond to different challenges, but you would probably get more from just talking to them. Most people anyway sit somewhere near the middle on the various dimensions – indeed to be at the extremes would, in Jung's own terms, be pathological – so fitting them into the boxes of a typology is inherently misleading.

Role	Characteristics
Coordinator	Confident, clear-headed, good delegator, may not be good team-worker.
Shaper	Energy and drive to move things forward, good under pressure, may not be tolerant of others.
Plant	Creative problem-solver, imaginative, may be poor communicator and impatient with practical details.
Monitor-evaluator	Good judgement, cool head, realistic and down to earth, but may de-energise project.
Implementer	Practical, efficient, organized, reliable, but may be slow to adapt to changes.
Resource investigator	Enthusiastic, can-do explorer and good communicator, but can be over-optimistic or have short attention span.
Team-worker	Good listener, cooperative, good people-skills, but can be indecisive or focus on team at expense of project.
Completer-finisher	Thorough, conscientious, perfectionist, but can be worrier and likely to be poor delegator.
Specialist	Brings particular knowledge or skills, but may struggle to relate those to wider project.

Belbin team roles (see *www.belbin.com* for more detail)

A rather different kind of analysis, focused more on people's behaviour than on their underlying psychology, is Meredith Belbin's empirically based team-role inventory. Belbin identified nine behavioural styles manifest in teamwork situations: coordinator or chairman, shaper, plant, monitor-evaluator, implementer, resource investigator, team worker, completer-finisher and specialist. The idea here is that people at work will gravitate towards the role or roles with which they are behaviourally most comfortable and will perform best in those roles. For a team to succeed, however, all the roles have to be covered by someone, so in putting a team together you will ideally want to pick people with a good balance of behavioural styles and one that covers reasonably effectively all the bases without getting so large as to be unwieldy. (Belbin suggests that four is generally the optimum size for a team, with larger groups losing the benefits of interpersonal team dynamics.) A team with three coordinators and no completer-finisher is unlikely to be very effective.

Perhaps because it's empirically derived and theory-light, Belbin's team-role inventory is one of the more useful techniques for managers. If you're putting a team together, your first thoughts will be about personality clashes and temperamental compatibility: can these people work together at all? But you also need to think about how effectively they can work together to deliver the goods, and the inventory is a useful aid. It's simple enough to be applied in the normal run of your job: just talk to people, as you should be doing anyway, about their strengths and weaknesses, the roles they prefer and the roles they shy away from. But it's not so simple as to be obvious. If you had to specify team roles for yourself, you wouldn't necessarily come up with these.

Techniques for organizational analysis tend to suffer from the same drawbacks as those for analysing people. Typically they are as much theories about how organizations might work as analyses of how they do work, and while they can raise fascinating questions, they don't generally give useful answers.

One of the more insightful models of how organizations work is Charles Handy's exploration of the 'gods of management'. Handy identified four basic approaches to managing, each of which he associated with one of the Greek gods. These approaches, he suggested, could be linked to individual preferences, but also to organizational cultures. Thus, one way of managing work (associated with Zeus, ruler of the gods) is through the exercise of personal power and interpersonal relationships, as in a small entrepreneurial organization. Another (associated with Apollo, god of reason) is through fixed offices or roles, as in a rationalized bureaucracy. A third is through the more fluid structuring of projects and tasks (Athena, the problem-solver). And a fourth is by not managing at all, by leaving people to get on with it, as happens in some creative or professional firms (Dionysus, the god of the self-oriented individual).

In practice, most organizations combine elements of more than one of these cultures, and there are often tensions between how people want to manage and how they want to be managed, as well as between established ways of managing and the ways of managing that may be needed when circumstances change. But the model provides a useful way in to exploring these tensions, understanding why things work the way they do, and how and why they sometimes don't work at all.

Looking at some of our examples, both Rick's restaurant and Brad's building firm are simple, top-down, entrepreneurial organizations (Zeus) and Belle's bank is a classic large bureaucracy (Apollo), at least in the retail banking side. The investment-banking division is characterized both by the roles, rules and procedures of a bureaucracy and by a cultural disposition to ignore them, as traders pursue their Dionysian self-interest. Melanie's hospital displays a similar clash of cultures. Doctors don't typically have the self-interest of financial traders, and we wouldn't normally think of them as Dionysian. Their focus is more Athenian, upon the medical task, the skills needed to achieve it, and upon bringing together and coordinating those skills in the way appropriate to each individual case. They prefer to manage this coordination themselves, however, and, like Dionysians, they are very resistant to being managed by others.

Ed's company too shows a mix of approaches. In general terms it is managed bureaucratically, and Ed's own ability to get things done stems in large part from the authority of his office. But the bureaucratic style isn't a good fit to research and development, or to the special projects that deliver highly customized solutions to individual clients, and in these areas there is a tension between the Apollonian task culture of the project and the underlying bureaucratic structures.

The danger with models like Handy's is that however much their authors stress that you shouldn't try to squeeze real organizations into 'ideal' types, the temptation is always to do that. The result is that you capture something important about your organization but at the same time close your eyes to other things that are also important. Two frameworks that largely avoid these problems, and are especially useful for managers, are Peter Checkland's soft systems methodology and Gerry Johnson's cultural web.

The idea behind soft systems methodology is that when organizations run up against problems, a big part of the problem is that the problem itself is not well defined. It depends who's looking at it and from what perspective. So we need to go back a step and analyse an organizational system not as an objective entity, but as a fusion of several subjectively perceived systems, which Checkland calls human activity systems. We need, in other words, to take account not only of what people are doing, but of what they think they are doing, and what they think other people are doing. As urged earlier in the book, we need to see things from other people's perspectives.

In its fully worked out form, soft systems methodology is a complex and sophisticated technique, but at its core there are just two main components. One is a way of defining a human activity system, as seen from a particular perspective. This is summarized by its CATWOE aspects. Who are the Clients the system is serving (and/or the victims or beneficiaries it is affecting)? Who are the Actors carrying out its activities? What are the Transformations it is effecting (from inputs to outputs, in the form of products or services)? What is the Worldview that makes sense of the systems' existence? Who are the Owners of the system? And what are the Environmental or External constraints that the system takes for granted?

The other is a mapping of the system, again from a particular perspective. A soft systems map looks very like the kind of value-added map described earlier. Draw a circle for each activity, with links and arrows wherever one activity depends on another. Only in this case what you are drawing is not necessarily how the system does work or how it should work, but how it appears to work from the viewpoint of a particular actor. So different actors may map the system in different ways, and they will also define its CATWOE attributes in different ways, depending on their particular perspectives.

Now, to use this as a general management tool, try drawing and defining the system from the perspectives of its key actors and key stakeholders. You will, of course, need to ask the actors how they perceive things. You may also need to be a bit of an amateur anthropologist and observe how they behave and how they respond to different situations. Because people take for granted their own viewpoints, they aren't always conscious of how those viewpoints are made up. But if you keep your mind open (and your eyes and

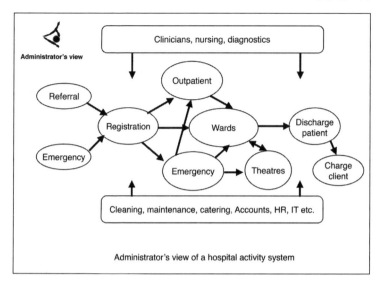

Administrator's view of a hospital activity system

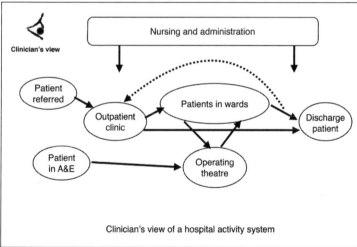

Clinician's view of a hospital activity system

ears), you will get a much richer view of the organization and how it really works, as opposed to how it is meant to work.

Soft systems analysis is hard to illustrate briefly, as its strength lies in bringing to light quite subtle differences of perspective, which can nevertheless make a significant difference. To give a very rough idea of how it can work, though, let's think about how Melanie's hospital might look from a couple of artificially exaggerated viewpoints. The first illustration portrays the hospital system as it might appear in the eyes of a senior administrator. The second shows how it might appear in the eyes of a consultant surgeon.

In terms of the CATWOE aspects, the administrator tends to see the main clients of the system as the primary trusts – mainly GP practices – who buy the hospital's services within the internal market of the UK National Health Service. For the surgeon, in contrast, the clients are the patients. The actors, for the administrator, are all of the hospital's staff, who come together in different combinations and different ways in the various scenes of activity – in the wards, the operating theatres, the administrative offices and so on. For the surgeon, the primary actors are the clinicians, supported by the nursing staff and perhaps the technicians and record keepers. Other people, out of sight or at least out of mind, are seen as peripheral to the system. Both administrator and surgeon see the system as transforming people in need of treatment to people satisfactorily treated, but again there is a difference of focus as the administrator sees treatments more in terms of statistics and the surgeon more in terms of people. There is little difference in world-view, with both committed to universal healthcare, and both see the system as owned, in some sense, by the community, but whereas the administrator sees this ownership as exercised through the Foundation Trust, the surgeon tends to see it as exercised through public-serving professionals. Finally, while the primary constraints, for the administrator, are financial, for the surgeon they are medical.

These pictures are artificial exaggerations, but we can see how people in different positions and with different values and experiences might see a complex system of this kind in quite different ways, and so have quite different versions of what is going on in any activity. Another doctor or another administrator might see things differently, and a laboratory analyst and an agency nurse might have different viewpoints again. And you can't fully understand how an organization works until you understand how the people in it think it works, and how they interpret their own contributions.

Soft systems methodology helps you to understand how people's viewpoints differ. The aim of a cultural web analysis is to understand the attitudes and assumptions that are widely shared and taken for granted, without thinking about them. Organizational cultures are typically built on the values and approaches of the organizations' founders and on recipes for success that have developed and become embedded over time. The ways of thinking they embody wouldn't have become established if they didn't work. But, once established, they are very hard to shift, and when circumstances change, cultures often don't, leaving organizations out of sync with the demands of their environments.

The cultural web was developed as a way of exposing the taken-for-granted attitudes and assumptions of an organization so as to highlight mismatches with the environment and provide a starting point for the discussion and management of change. Like soft systems methodology, however, it can be a useful management tool, even when there are no particular problems to be addressed. The basic idea is to probe into the most central and most deeply embedded features of the culture by starting from its more visible manifestations. These include the organizational structure of the organization; its monitoring and control systems; its incentive systems; its communications practices (email, phone, formal reports, etc.); its rituals and routines (everything from staff induction to strategic planning, from ways of developing the business to ways of taking coffee breaks); the stories people tell (of success or failure, or of particular groups of people); the symbols and artefacts found around the place (buildings, offices, dress codes); and its power structures, both formal and informal (where does the real power lie).

It doesn't really matter in which category you put an observation, the point is to open up and start thinking about what is valued in the organization and how it works. The end point, at the centre of the web, is what is called the organizational paradigm: what do all

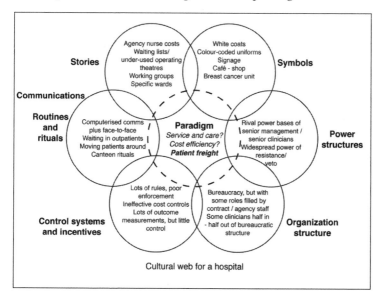

Cultural web for a hospital

these things point to? In a nutshell, how do we do things around here? That's unlikely to be stated explicitly, but it's very useful to know!

To illustrate this, let's stick with the hospital. The illustration shows the cultural web for Melanie's hospital (every hospital will be different, of course, and this is not meant to be typical). Some of the entries are self-explanatory; others are shorthand for observations that will be meaningful to the staff, patients and others involved. So, for example, under rituals, 'waiting in outpatients' refers to the practice of setting appointment times for patients an hour before the surgery even starts, so as to make absolutely sure they are there on time. 'Moving patients around' refers to the way they are labelled and sent from one department to another, joining a new queue each time.

Under stories, the reference to 'agency nurse costs' refers to the habit of cutting core staffing to save money and then spending £2,000 to £3,000 a week on agency nurses to fill the gaps. Operating theatres are under-used because of clashes of shift times and working procedures, even though there are large waiting-lists. Working groups are set up to solve these kinds of problems, but fail to make progress and never report. In some specific parts of the hospital, however, things seem to work wonderfully well. All these are stories. They are not necessarily true stories, indeed they are often grossly exaggerated, but they are based on some underlying truths and their very existence tells us something about the hospital and about what people are trying to do, as well as about what they may be failing to do.

The physical symbols of a culture can be hard to identify and hard to interpret, but some that stand out here are the colour-coded uniforms for nurses, auxiliaries, porters and so on; the signage, which is more like a labelling of parts than anything that might help people find their way around; and the new café-shop area that feels like an airport transit terminal. The breast cancer unit, built as part of a government initiative, stands out because it is a new build and quite different from the main hospital: comfortable, user-friendly and truly efficient.

What the cultural web leads you to is an organization's paradigm or 'how things are done round here' and, like many organizations, the hospital is confused. There are two competing versions of what it should be doing: providing personal service and care, and providing cost-efficient treatment. But what it is doing, much of the time, is moving patients around like freight or like components in a factory – not what anyone ever intended.

MANAGING THE SELF

Managing yourself is arguably the hardest of all challenges for a manager. It's also the one in which you can get least help, either from other people or from tools and techniques. There are three main parts to the problem: time, attention and well-being. Managing your time is a problem because, in a managerial role, there's never enough of it. Managing your attention is a problem because there are too many things to attend to and too many distractions. Managing your well-being is a problem because the responsibilities of managing tend to bring with them stresses. The three are obviously linked in a vicious or virtuous circle. If you're feeling stressed, you will find it harder to focus your attention and everything will take longer – which will make it all the more stressful. If you're on top and focused, you will feel good and it will be easier to stay on top and focused.

There are many techniques for time management, but all boil down to disciplines for listing, prioritizing and chunking activities. The worst possible situation to find yourself in is getting nothing done because there's so much to be done and you can't get your head round it, so most techniques start with a simple to-do list of activities and associated deadlines. Large or amorphous tasks are best split up into manageable chunks. The risk otherwise is that a task that would be quite achievable if systematically planned and executed over time may become unachievable, or land you in a crisis, if you put off the whole thing until the deliverable becomes urgent. So you spend a little time planning or mapping out the activities involved and apply deadlines and priorities to each part.

You then take all the activities in your list and classify them according to their urgency and importance – then you get ruthless. If you are under time pressure and something is not important, you just don't do it. Never mind if it's something you wouldn't mind doing or would enjoy doing: it's not important and you haven't time. You may be able to delegate it to someone else. You may possibly keep it on a list of things to do when you do have time on your hands, but that's not usually a good idea – it keeps hanging on in your mind and takes up time, even though you never do it. Again, if it's really bugging you and it won't take too long, you may be best just to do it and get it out of the way – perhaps even get rid of it before it makes the list. It's generally the case, after all, that 80 per cent of your tasks can be done in just 20 per cent of the time needed to do them all, and getting rid of those 80 per cent may help you to focus on the 20 per cent. But most things take much longer than you expect and, if you don't have enough time, why are you spending it on things that aren't important? It comes down in the end to your own psychology, but it's generally best just to cross things off the list. Don't worry if they're done or not – forget them.

You are now left with the important tasks, broken down and prioritized in time, and your main challenge is to discipline yourself to stick with that prioritization. It's always tempting to do some things, even though they're not urgent, as a way of unconsciously putting off other, more difficult or less enjoyable things, even though they are urgent. Avoid the temptation and, if you've still got more to do than you can fit in, use the 80/20 principle as it should be used: as saying that 20 per cent of the effort will produce 80 per cent of the effective result. If you can't do everything, or think that you might not be able to do everything, do first what's most productive, for your unit and the organization.

All of this is much easier said than done, but you can be greatly helped by some general rules about how to approach your work. First, if you're overloaded already, say 'No'. In most organizations, a few people carry the bulk of the load, partly because they're willing and partly because they're competent. They become the go-to people when something needs to be done. But, if you keep taking on more things, however competent you may be, your competence will suffer. The solution to the problem is to build up other people's competence and willingness, not to try and do everything yourself.

Second, don't waste time by overworking. Nobody can work twenty-four hours a day. Very few people can work twelve hours a day, for more than a few months at a stretch, without a serious drop in performance. People vary in their individual capacities, but many managers would achieve more if they worked shorter hours. There comes a point when the extra hours put in are not really productive, and soon after that a point is reached where all you are doing is wearing yourself out so that your whole day becomes unproductive.

Third, you can extend your capacity by managing your energy and concentration levels. When you're tired, take a break. If at all practicable, take a siesta. Get some fresh air. Take regular exercise. Take regular holidays. Don't just keep taking caffeine. And don't worry that in doing this you are using up valuable time. If there's one overriding rule of time management it is to treat time as something you can manage, to look at things from outside time, so to speak, and not allow yourself to be swept along, as if completely powerless, by time's tide.

At this point, the techniques of time management begin to merge with those of attention management and general well-being. One of the ways you save on time is by optimizing the way you use that time, by maintaining your focus and concentration, and to do this you need to be refreshed and in good shape. Managing attention is also important in its own right, however, as we noted earlier when discussing the need for 'quality time' for planning and moral attentiveness.

The ability to focus on the problem in hand and shut out everything else is a tremendous asset for managing, but it's not easy to acquire. Some people seem naturally good at it. Some people can even switch their brains from one task to another in a split-second, perhaps turning on and off a problem while holding a conversation on something completely different. Generally, people who have had a rigorous education – in maths, science or languages, say – will have learnt to concentrate better than others, as will people who have trained in the military, or played chess, or played other games and sports that require high levels of attention and focus.

If you've not had these benefits, learning to manage your attention as an adult manager is a tall order, but there are techniques you can use. Many games and sports, if played seriously, also require intense concentration, and if you can capture the state of mind you adopt in such circumstances, you can try consciously to reproduce it when addressing a problem at work. Meditation techniques and associated physical exercise like tai chi and yoga can teach you to still your mind and empty it of its usual clutter. When you start meditation, it may take you ages to get anywhere at all, but once you reach a certain, quite basic, level, you should be able to use it routinely, in fairly short stretches, to clear your head in the morning or even in the middle of the day. As discussed earlier in the book, you can also teach yourself to use cues (a cup of tea, a visual image) to calm and reset your mind when it is muddled.

Of course, people who go in for meditation aren't usually thinking about doing better at work. They are thinking about their general well-being. But the two are inseparable. If you are well, you will generally work well. If you are stressed or unwell, your work will suffer along with everything else. So, to use the phrase beloved of parents, you should always 'look after yourself'. Eat properly and, above all, sleep properly. And if you see signs of stress – if you start suffering from unexplained physical pains or twitches, if you find that you're not noticing your surroundings, if you find it difficult to relax, or if your friends and loved ones feel the tension in the air – then act.

Physical exercise is often the best response (maybe you used to jog but stopped because you didn't have time...), because it turns the pent-up stress energy into productive, physical energy. If you have a hobby that you use to relax – painting, gardening, whatever – make sure you use it. (Again you've probably stopped as a result of the pressures, and stopping has made them worse.) Talk things through with somebody and you may be able to work out what it is that's stressing you, or at least where the stress is coming from (identifying a more precise cause can be difficult, if not impossible), and whether it's manageable. Certainly you will get further talking with someone, anyone, than trying to think it out for yourself, because one of the main symptoms of stress is that you can't think straight on your own. If the source of the stress is at work and if you have holiday owing, then take it, and do something to get away from work – with your family, with friends. And if you conclude that things are not going to get better, then take the decision to quit and start looking for another job, while you're still in a fit state to land one.

All this is really common sense but it's very hard to do, so you really need to force yourself, and the way you can best do this is by anticipating it. Start out with the assumption that work may get stressful, and that whatever the cost, you won't let it get on top of you: that the job has to work for you, not you for it. Look out for any signs of trouble, and be prepared to act before you get into a downward spiral. This is not just a sensible precaution. It also frees you up to relax and really enjoy what you're doing – and when approached in the right way, there are few things quite so enjoyable as managing!

Glossary: Essential Jargon

The tools and techniques we have covered so far are among the most useful for everyday managing, but there are, of course, many more and some of them have found their way into everyday management-speak. Some people refer to them as a way of establishing their personal credentials, to show that they are management-savvy. Others have become familiar with them at business school and continue to use them back at work, taking it for granted that they will be understood. It is useful to have at least heard of some of these, and to have a very rough idea of what people are talking about, even if you don't know any of the details. You can then nod politely when they come up, not embarrass yourself by displaying ignorance and check them out later, if appropriate. There are many books giving concise accounts of all the best-known theories, concepts, frameworks, models and techniques, and in all cases Wikipedia and other online sources will give you enough information to tell if you need or want to go further. All we shall give here is a kind of glossary, a few lines on each to indicate what it is about.

7-S framework   A framework for business analysis devised by Tom Peters and Robert Waterman at McKinsey. It covers the Strategy, Structure, Systems, Staff, Styles, Skills and Superordinate goals (values, ideals and objectives) of the organization.

Activity based costing (ABC)   An approach to management accounting that attempts to allocate all costs, including appropriate shares of overhead costs, to the particular activities of an organization.

Ansoff matrix   A simple classification of marketing strategies according to whether you are dealing with new or existing products and new or existing strategies.

Balanced scorecard   An approach to performance management developed by Robert Kaplan and David Norton that measures performance according to a relatively wide range of key performance indicators. These are derived, through a more or less complex methodology, from an analysis of the organization's overall goals and specific strategic objectives.

Belbin role inventory   A classification of behavioural styles within teamwork.

Boston box (or BCG matrix)   A technique devised by the Boston Consulting Group for analysing the profitability and prospects of different business or product lines within a diversified company. Businesses are rated according to their current market share and the rate of market growth, and classified as stars (high share, high growth: invest); cash cows (high share, low growth: milk); question marks (low share, high growth: build share or get out); and dogs (low share, low growth: just get out).

Business process re-engineering   An approach to improving efficiency by taking apart business processes and rebuilding them from scratch, along the lines of scientific management, but making use of state-of-the-art IT.

Core competence   A term used by Gary Hamel and C. K. Prahalad to describe a distinctive framework of skills and technologies that penetrate every aspect of an organization and can be used as the basis for a range of different businesses.

Cultural web   A tool devised by Gerry Johnson for exploring the culture of an organization.

Experience curve   A description of the fact that the cost and time spent making or doing something will go down over time as a function of the total number of units you have already made or the number of times you have done it. Not to be confused with economies of scale, which arise from making things in large batches.

Five forces   According to Michael Porter, the sets of factors that influence the overall profitability of an industry: the barriers to entry, the rivalry amongst existing competitors (affected, among other things, by the balance of market share and the barriers to exit), the bargaining powers of customers and suppliers and the threat posed by substitute products. These all describe market inefficiencies, without which owners would switch their resources to where profits were highest, leading to all industries having the same profit levels.

Gantt chart   A chart named after Henry Gantt and used in product planning, that assigns tasks to slots in a calendar.

Generic strategies   A model due to Michael Porter, who argues that viable competitive strategies must be located at the ends of two dimensions – cost versus differentiation and broad versus focused – and not stuck in the middle. The underlying intuition is that for customers to buy your product, it must be either the cheapest or the best (in terms of their needs), but that firms can rarely pursue low cost and high quality objectives at once.

Groupthink   A term coined by Irving Janis to describe a phenomenon in which a desire to avoid conflict and reach consensus results in groups overlooking key considerations, sidelining their critical faculties and making irrational decisions.

Hawthorne studies   Experiments carried out by Elton Mayo, a key figure in the inter-war Human Relations movement. They suggested that performance levels in a factory owed less to the optimization of conditions and more to the human aspects of leadership and team dynamics.

Internal rate of return (IRR)   An alternative to net present value for estimating the financial viability of a project. IRR is the effective annual rate of return on a project, which can be compared with the return that would be achieved by simply investing the money safely. It equates to the discount rate at which the net present value would be zero.

Key performance indicators (KPIs)   Measures on which important aspects of the performance in an activity can be judged.

Management by objectives (MBO)   A management approach formulated by Peter Drucker based on agreed management targets, in which performance measurement is used as a means to self-improvement and self-control. It attempts to combine the efficiency elements of scientific management with the general assumptions of Theory Y.

Marketing mix   The different dimensions of marketing, usually categorized in terms of the 4 Ps: Product, Price, Promotion and Place (or distribution), sometimes extended to 5 or 7 Ps. More customer-oriented versions stress 4 (or more) Cs: Customer needs, Cost, Communication and Convenience.

Maslow's hierarchy of needs   A proposed ranking of human needs, from the basic physiological needs through security, love, esteem and self-actualization to self-transcendence. Herbert Maslow argued that the most basic levels had to be satisfied before the higher ones could motivate people, and that once the needs at the lower levels were satisfied, they no longer acted as motivators.

Milgram experiments   A famous set of experiments, conducted by Stanley Milgram, in which volunteers were instructed by a 'scientist' to raise the electric charge apparently being administered to a 'subject' (both in fact actors), as part of a 'learning experiment', up to lethal levels – and they largely complied. Variously interpreted as evidence of unquestioning belief in authority or of a failure to cope when a situation makes no sense.

Myers Briggs analysis   A technique for classifying people according to their psychological types.

Net present value (NPV)   The effective value today of future revenue streams less present and future costs, where allowance is made for the fact that money held and safely invested would grow in value in the future.

Pareto principle (80/20 rule)   The principle that 80 per cent of the outcome or output of a process can generally be attributed to 20 per cent of the source or input. For example: 80 per cent of revenues to 20 per cent of products; 80 per cent of personal output to 20 per cent of time spent; 80 per cent of profits to 20 per cent of customers; 80 per cent of computer crashes to 20 per cent of bugs; 80 per cent of wealth to 20 per cent of population.

PEST (or STEP) analysis   A simple approach to the analysis of the competitive or organizational environment in terms of four main classes of event, factor, situation or future possibility: Political, Economic, Social and Technological.

Scenario planning   A technique for creative long-range planning in the face of major uncertainty. Also useful more generally for opening your mind to the variety of possible futures.

Scientific management   A rational approach to management due to Frederick Winslow Taylor and based on the division of labour into specialized tasks and the optimization of both the physical movements of workers and the machinery they use. More generally applied to all work systems based on time-and-motion studies and strict control of the workers.

Six sigma   A technique for improving the efficiency of manufacturing processes and the quality of the goods they produce by identifying and removing the sources of variability that result in defective products or delays.

SMART   A mnemonic used to identify appropriate project objectives. They should be: Strategic, Measurable, Agreed, Realistic and Timed.

Soft systems methodology   A way of analysing the activity systems of organizations by looking at them from the subjective viewpoints of different actors.

SWOT analysis   A simple approach to strategic analysis that entails identifying the Strengths and Weaknesses of the firm or organization and the Opportunities and Threats posed by its (changing) environment. A good strategy capitalizes on the strengths and opportunities, and neutralizes the weaknesses and threats.

Theory X and Theory Y   These terms were coined by Douglas McGregor to characterize two contrasting sets of assumptions underlying management practice. Theory X assumes that people will avoid working if they can, prefer to be told what to do, and can only be made productive through coercion and control. Theory Y assumes that work comes naturally and is a source of satisfaction, that people are motivated by self-actualization, and that they are capable of creativity, self-direction and autonomous responsibility.

Transformational leadership   A style of leadership based on actively inspiring, enabling and motivating people, rather than on rewards and punishments. Transformational leaders also act as role models, show concern for their followers and encourage creativity.

Triple bottom line (or 3BL)   An approach to accounting that includes the social and environmental results of an organization, as well as its financial results (the usual 'bottom line' of profit or loss). A 3BL company accounts publicly for how it treats employees and communities (its corporate social responsibility) and for its impact on the environment (in terms of carbon use, waste management, etc.)

Value chain analysis   A group of techniques for analyzing how an organization achieves competitive success by adding customer value.

Index